Understanding Cat Behaviour

BY

DR. GORDON ROBERTS BVSC MRCVS

Table of Contents

Introduction

Chapter One – Vocalisations

Chapter Two – Body Language

Chapter Three – Socialisation

Chapter Four – Righting Reflex

Chapter Five – Scent Spraying and Rubbing

Chapter Six – Body Posture

Chapter Seven – Eating and Drinking

Chapter Eight – Kneading

Chapter Nine – Feline Intelligence

Chapter Ten – Human Behaviour Influences

Chapter Eleven – Indoor and Outdoor Cats

Chapter Twelve – Adolescent and Senior Cats

Chapter Thirteen – Dealing With Difficult Behaviour

Chapter Fourteen – Behaviour Training Tips

Chapter Fifteen - The Myths of Cat Behaviour

Chapter Sixteen – Frequently Asked Questions on Cat Behaviour

Conclusion

Resources

Hello! My name is Gordon Roberts and I'm the author of this book. I hope you enjoy all of the specialist advice it contains. I'm a huge advocate of preventative care for animals, and I'd love to see more pet owners taking the time to research their pet's health care needs.

Being proactive and educating yourself about your pet's health now, rather than later on, could save you and your pet a lot of trouble in the long run.

If you'd like to read more of my professional pet care advice simply go to my website at http://drgordonroberts.com/freereportsdownload/.

As a thank you for purchasing this book, you'll find dozens of bonus pet care reports there to download and keep, absolutely free of charge!

Best wishes,
Gordon
Founder, Wellpets

Introduction

Cats are unique creatures with many behaviors that people find interesting. Whether you're listening to the variety of their vocalisations or watching them landon their feet after a fall, their behavior is definitely intriguing. Cats are not the social creatures that dogs are, but they have their own ways of interacting with other cats, other animals and people. Some of these interactions are so subtle as to go unnoticed by humans, unless you know for what you are looking. It will help to learn more about cats and their behavior, if you want to more fully understand these unique animals.

Cats have their own ways of marking territory, and even their people. Your catmay have rubbed her face along the side of your hand, and if she does this with her mouth involved, she may be marking you as her own person. It's not like a slobbery dog kiss, but she is letting you know that you are hers, and cat fans find this appealing in its own way. You'll never know everything your cat is thinking, since she is a creature unlike any other. Cats will never be an open book for humans, but perhaps that is one of the reasons we find cats so interesting.

CHAPTER 1
VOCALISATIONS
~

Cats have a unique type of Vocalisation used to communicate with other cats and with their people, as well. When you share your home with a cat or cats, you should become familiar with the sounds and nuances of your individual cats' vocabularies.

When your cat speaks to you, you need to know whether she is fearful, playful or simply hungry. Once you learn her language, you can share more of your cat's life and be a bigger part of that life.

Domestic cats are believed to develop more sophisticated language patterns as compared to feral and wild cats. Perhaps that is because some of their language is used to converse with us.

Meow
This is the sound most often associated with cats, but some cats never make this exact sound. Whatever the variation, your cat usually uses a meow as a greeting, either to you or to other cats.

Mew
Kittens mew when they want attention from their mothers. A mew will become louder if your cat is fearful, or in distress. Some cats mew instead of making the more typical "meow" that people use to describe general cat language.

Chirp
Chirps are high-pitched, short sounds that cats often use to express their anticipation of receiving something they enjoy. This may mean a treat, affection, or playtime. Chirps are sometimes used to get attention.

Purring
The purr is a motor-like, vibrating sound that humans associate with contentment. Actually, it may also be used by a cat to comfort herself if she is in pain or experiencing anxiety. Veterinarians have noticed cats purring when they are in pain, so it is believed that cats use the purring to soothe themselves. Mother cats typically purr to their kittens to give them security and comfort. The subtle or strong vibrations are also helpful for kittens to use to find their mother in her nest. Newborn kittens cannot hear or see, so they can feel mother near through vibration.

Growl
There is no mistaking a growl when you hear one. It is usually a simple warning before a cat gets violent. It may also be used to scare off a perceived foe before it comes to violence. Some cats become possessive of their food, and may growl at an interloper who might want to steal some of it.

Chirrup
This is also called a trill. It is a sound that incorporates purring and meowing. It is usually a very happy sound and is sometimes used as a greeting.

Hiss
This sound brings to mind those made by snakes. It usually only lasts several seconds. It is a warning to others to stay away. It may be loud or quiet, depending on the cat and the circumstances. Hissing can help a cat who is low in the pecking order become more respected if it is believed to be serious by her cat compatriots.

Spit
A spit is a very short sound that sounds like popping. It is especially vocal if the entrance of another cat startles your kitty. Spitting may be heard before or after hissing, and often times the spit will be used just before a cat runs away. This is especially true with cats that are naturally timid.

Squeak
This sound is high-pitched and raspy, and is usually made when your cat anticipates that something good is coming. Treats or meals may elicit squeaks. Sometimes cats also squeak when they are playing.

Shriek
This is a high-pitched, harsh sound that is used in aggression or in painful situations. You are most likely to hear a cat shriek when she is fighting another cat. It can be a scary sound, especially since is not typically heard that often.

Caterwaul
This is an awful sound and is made by mating cats. You may hear it late at night close to your home. Spayed and neutered cats make better pets and you won't have to listen to this sound, at least in your home, if your cats are fixed.

Murmur
Murmuring sounds a bit like a trill or chirrup. It is a quiet, soft sound that is made with your cat's mouth closed. Mother cats murmur to their young. It may be used as part of a greeting ritual by your cat when you come home from work. In this case, it is often followed by purring and rubbing.

Silent Meow
This is one of the most intriguing of Vocalisations, but it technically may not be a Vocalisation at all. The motion for meowing is made with the mouth, but there is no sound. Some people believe that this sound may be of a pitch that is too high for humans to hear. Silent meows are wonderful, even though they are noiseless.

Chatter

This is an "ack-ack" type of sound that is softly uttered when your cat sees a bird or squirrel outside a window. There may be almost no sound actually heard. Humans believe the chatter means that their cat is frustrated, but only the cats know for sure.

Moan

Moaning is low, mournful and sad, and is sometimes heard just before your cat coughs or vomits. Elderly cats may make the sound if they are lost. When used in the presence of people, it usually means that your cat needs your help, or at least your reassurance.

Vocal Variations among Cats

These Vocalisations are generalised and not all cats sound the same when they make the same titled noise. Some sounds have more than one meaning, depending on the situation and cat involved. You probably hear your cat talk during the day and know exactly what she means.

Kitten mews are among the friendliest of cat sounds, generally of a higher tone than some of the more unpleasant sounds they may make later in life. The vocal pattern and tone of sounds made by cats indicate whether the cat is feeling friendly or decidedly unfriendly.

Friendly cat sounds are usually higher on the tonal scale and they move from high notes to low. Sounds made with friendly intent are usually shorter in duration than angry or fretful sounds. Sounds made by urgent cats move from lower to higher ranges. The sound may increase in volume if your cat is angry or upset.

Cats and Their People

Cats who have outgoing and friendlydispositions are often quite vocal with their chosen people. Your cat may string together various friendly sounds, as though she is forming sentences to speak with you. She probably expects that you will talk back.

Some cats may be perfectly friendly and happy, but simply not as vocal. These cats are more likely to use body language to let you know what they want. You can almost converse without words, once a non-vocal cat lets you know her signs.

Just because your cat doesn't talk doesn't mean she doesn't want you to speak to her. She probably will enjoy your voice even if she is not talkative herself.

Even cats in the same family will commonly develop different Vocalisations and vocabularies. You may have two sisters from the same litter, and one may be quite vocal, while the other makes more use of body language than voice. Some cats greet you with a "hello" meow when they enter the room, and some won't. Those that don't speak will usually rub on you or otherwise communicate with you.

Your cat may be more likely to speak with you if you speak to her often. It's not a guarantee, but she may feel more like speaking if you are an active participant in the conversations. Cats get a feeling of security from hearing your voice. The tone and cadence you use with your cat can mimic that of mothers talking to human babies. The rhythm and tone is the same, and is nurturing and calming to hear.

Since cats are small and dependent on you for their care, speaking to them with a calm and supportive voice is natural, and it is healthy for your cats. Cats will bring out your parental instincts, whether you have children or not.

CHAPTER TWO
BODY LANGUAGE
~

Even if her Vocalisations do not fully tell you how your cat is feeling about something or someone, her body language will. Cats use many signals, including facial expressions and body posturing, which convey their message and help them in avoiding confrontations. When you learn about feline posture, you can deepen your bond with your cat and prevent the misunderstanding of her expressions.

The "Halloween" Cat Pose
You've probably seen cardboard and plastic cats made for the witching season. The cat has her back arched and looks very defensive. This isn't just a mythical pose. Your cat's tail tells you a lot about her mood. When she holds her tail high, it means that she is confident. If

it curls around your leg, it signals her friendliness towards you. When it is tucked between or below the legs, it means that your cat is anxious or insecure.

The full-fur, upright tail means your cat feels threatened. If you combine that with an arched back and hair that is upright along her spine, this means "Back off". Your cat probably never uses this position with you, but she may with unfamiliar cats or other animals or people.

The Relaxed Cat
Your cat, when relaxed, has ears at rest or pointed slightly forward and to the side. This position indicates that she is content and feels neither aggressive nor fearful. She may even roll over on her back when you pet her, and this means she is quite relaxed. In other circumstances, the rollover may mean other things. However, if she is quite comfortable with you, she may be looking for a tummy rub.

Cat Eyes
Many cats find direct stares to be threatening, depending on the situation. In a social setting, your cat may seek out a person who is ignoring her. She perceives his inattention as a non-threatening gesture.

When your cat becomes fearful, her pupils expand. This allows them to take in the most information, visually, about a situation. If your cat's eyes have pupils fully dilated, she is probably quite frightened, and may wish to retreat.

In angry or aroused cats, the pupil often narrows or constricts, which helps cats to focus on important details. Your cat's eyes also respond to indoor or outdoor lighting, so narrow pupils may simply mean that there is a good deal of light in the area.

Cat Ear Movements
If your cat is nervous or agitated, her ears are probably twitching. She may be looking for reassurance if she is nervous, so offer it to her. Medical issues may also lead to persistent ear twitching, so take your cat to the vet if you suspect this might be the problem.

When your cat is interested and alert, or if something captures her attention, her ears will usually be straight up. Her posture will also be forward. Your cat probably greets you with her ears erect, and this is a friendly greeting.

Ears can also signal aggression. If your cat's ears move from forward to backward, her sense of aggression has been activated. Ears moving from upright to horizontal usually indicate submissiveness, annoyance or fear. If your cat's ears are often horizontal, she may have ear mites or an ear infection, so have that checked out by your veterinarian.

When your cat's ears are flattened against her head, it doesn't take a body language expert to see that she is probably frightened and may move to attack. Her ears are held this way instinctively when she fights, to protect them from teeth and claws.

If you are unfamiliar with a cat, ears laid back means that you should not try to touch her or pick her up. This could lead to being scratched or bitten.

The Body of the Cat
Your cat's body tells you a lot about how she is feeling. If her back is arched, she is probably angry or frightened. If it is only arched a bit, and there is no hair standing up, she may be welcoming your friendly touch.

If your cat lies on her back while purring or languishing in the sun, this indicates that she is quite relaxed. If she is lying on her back but is also growling, it could mean that she is very upset and getting ready to strike. If your cat rubs her chin against you, she is marking her territory, in a more pleasant way than you may have heard of this being done. She does this with doorways and toys that are hers, too.

Head Position
The position of your cat's head tells you several things. When she stretches her head forward, she is trying to see a human or feline facial expression, or trying to encourage touch. It is normally a friendly position.

When your cat is in conflict, she may raise her head if she is confident or assertive, but aggressiveness usually results in a lowering of the head. A submissive or inferior cat may also lower her head. However, inferior cats that are in defensive mode may raise their heads.

If your cat has her head down and turns her head to the side to avoid eye contact, this is usually indicative of a lack of interest. Your cat also perceives something non-threatening if she uses this posture. When she is relaxed, she may pull her chin in.

Kneading of Paws
Kneading is sometimes known as "making biscuits". It's easy to see where it got this name. When your cat kneads her claws, on you or the bed, for instance, it is held over from her life as a kitten. This is how nursing kittens massage their mother's teats to start the flow of milk. Usually, a cat is contented and happy when she kneads her claws.

The Playful Cat
When your cat is feeling playful, she has her pupils dilated a bit, her whiskers and ears forward and her tail up. Playing for a cat is a use of her hunting prowess. She may stalk a toy or you, in play, and crouch with her back end slightly higher than usual. Her bottom may wiggle a little, and then she will pounce. Then your cat will grasp her toy and bite it a little, wrestle with it on the floor, and kick out at it with her back feet. This means she just killed her toy. She may play with your proffered hand in the same way.

Flehman Response
When your cat is smelling something, she may lift her head, open her mouth a bit, curl her lips back and squint her eyes. This helps her to gather additional information about the object or person she is sniffing. The sense of smell is essential for your cat. She actually has an extra organ in her olfactory system that is shared with that of the horse. It is known as the Jacobson's organ. It is found on the roof of her mouth, behind her front teeth. It is fully connected to the nasal cavity. If your cat smells something that interests her, she will open her mouth and inhale. This sends scent molecules over this olfactory organ. It intensifies the odor and gives her more information about the object or person.

CHAPTER THREE
SOCIALISATION
~

What Is Feline Socialisation?

Feline Socialisation normally takes place during the earliest weeks of a kitten's life. In this process, she will learn to interact properly with cats, other animals and people. She will have many experiences with the world around her, so she will become accustomed to the sounds, sights and smells that she will encounter into adulthood.

Like many young animals, kittens accomplish Socialisation easily, until they have reached a certain age. When they have reached the end of this period, they become more naturally wired to be suspicious of new things. This is an important part of a cat's life. The fearless and open nature of young kittens allows them to become more comfortable with things and people that they will encounter every day in their adult life.

The suspiciousness beginning after the end of Socialisation ensures that he will be cautious with new things. New animals or things in his environment may be dangerous, and after she has learned about Socialisation, she learns that she must also be wary of some things in her world.

Socialise Your Kitten

If you have a kitten that is still young, it's important to utilise the period of Socialisation to introduce her to new things. This will allow her to become more comfortable as a companion animal that lives in a world of humans. This world includes many things and many people, including sights, smells, noises and sensations.

When should you socialise your kitten?
She will be most respective to your Socialisation studies when she is between the weeks of two and seven. As long as she is handled a lot and enjoys pleasing interactions with people and other animals, she will likely remain a cat who is friendly to other animals and humans as she grows. In addition, new experiences will stress her less if she is socialised during the proper time.

If your kitten does not have social contact with other animal and people before she is eight or nine weeks old, she may be fearful of people and new animals for her whole life. Likewise, if you try to tame an unsocialised, feral adult cat, it will be similar to working with any wild animal. Feral cats can become more tolerant of you if they see you a lot, but they won't be social animals like socialised domestic cats.

∼

Do Not Separate Kittens from Their Mother for Socialisation

∼

Early handling and exposure to the environment is beneficial for kittens, but you should not separate them from their mother while they are young. Mother cats pass on social skills to their kittens, and if you wean your kittens at too young an age, they may have difficulty in relating to other animals.

If your kittens and their mother cat have a good home, simply handle them to give them that human interaction, without removing them from Mama's care. If you are adopting a kitten from a litter which hasn't had any proper Socialisation, six or seven weeks of age is an optimal time. This will give you a chance to expose your kitten to many new things, and allow her to become used to people.

How Do You Properly Socialise YourKitten?
If you have the mother cat along with her litter, you need to help her to socialise the kittens. Get started at an early age, so that the kittens will become comfortable with people. Careful socialising of kittens will help them to mature into well-adjusted, wonderful pets.

The more contact with humans that kittens get before they are seven week old, the friendlier they are likely to be as they grow up. Kittens who are stroked and held even for just several minutes a day will begin exploring their world sooner and be less wary of strangers and unusual events later in their lives.

If Mama Kitty is all right with you being around her litter, you can even handle newborn kittens daily. Pick them up gently, stroke them softy and place them back in the nest. Handling sessions should be short. You don't want to over-stimulate the kittens or make them uncomfortable with people. If your Mama Kitty is overprotective of her littler, perhaps you can handle the kittens for just a few minutes while the mother leaves for meals or litter box stops.

Once your kittens are full alert, with ears and eyes open and working well, and they can regulate their body temperature, they can start to meet new people and experience new things. This usually happens between three and four weeks. Handle them daily, and expose them to new sensations, smells, sounds and sights.

When your kittens are on solid food, their mother may kill prey and bring it to her family. This helps the kittens to become interested in chasing objects and pouncing on them. You can use interactive toys at this time. This is also a good time to expose your kittens to various surfaces, like grass, concrete, gravel, linoleum and carpeting.

Give Your Kittens Objects to Explore

- Use paper bags, toys, packing paper and cardboard boxes for your kittens to play inside. This will allow them to learn about investigating various places with their little paws.
- Use different toys and bags so that they won't get bored. Scratching posts will be fun for them, too.
- Exposing young kittens to new experiences is an important factor in their growth, but don't overwhelm them.
- Petting them gently for a few minutes a day will help in the development of their social skills. Even small input of a visual tactile and auditory nature will help them with social skills, problem solving and coordination as they mature.
- Three or four weeks of age will be a good time to start the introduction of toys to your kittens. Attach toys to wands or strings so they can skitter like birds or mice. Tempting toys will exercise and entertain kittens, and teach them hunting lessons, too.
- Be sure to teach your kittens that human toes and fingers are not toys. Play biting is cute when kittens are young but not as much when they are older. Redirect kittens if they want to bite you during play sessions.

Take Your Kittens Out into the World

Many cats only experience travel as cramped carriers and sticks with needles at the veterinary clinic. Kittens should be taken out and even taken to kitten classes to improve their Socialisation skills.

Kitten classes are rapidly spreading, and are a great way to introduce your kittens to other cats and other people. Kitten Socialisation classes usually include just a few sessions. They may be held in the office of a veterinarian.

Your kittens will need to be vaccinated first, as well as de-wormed and tested negatively for FeLV/FIV. During these classes, your kittens will meet new people while you learn more about cat health and behavior. They also give your cat a chance for a car ride that ends in a pleasant environment.

What If Your Cat Wasn't Properly Socialised While Young?
If your cat or kitten was not socialised when she was young, you can still help her to function more easily in the world. It isn't impossible to help older cats become more comfortable with their surroundings. It may take longer, though. If your cat is shy, she may become comfortable eventually with people close to you. However, fearful adult cats won't be as social. Feral cats are even more difficult to socialise, and it's wise to seek out advice from an animal behaviorist if you adopt a semi-wild cat.

Introducing a New Kitten to Your Home

In basic feline hierarchy, a new kitten will not be dominant over an adult cat you already have. Separate the existing pet andthe new kitten for a couple days. Your adult cat will hear the kitten in the other room, and become more accustomed to the smell and sounds of the new kitten.

The next step is putting your new kitten in a carrier in the middle of a room, to give the two cats a chance to sniff each other. Do not be surprised if your adult cat bats at the cage, in a show of dominance. There may be hissing, too.

During the time you separate the cats, and afterwards, give them both plenty of attention. Keep them separated until they have accepted each other. Once they are comfortable loose and in the same room, lavish attention on the adult cat, too, so there won't be issues with jealousy.

Socialising Adult Cats

Adult cats are less flexible in adapting to new routines or new pets in the home. It's understandable considering that a cat, who has had all of your attention, suddenly has to share with another cat, or a dog. Introduce your cat to the smell of the new kitten. Give her a blanket that the new kitten has slept on. Let her spend time sniffing it, so she becomes accustomed to the scent of the new kitten.

Once they know each other, feeding from separate bowls is a good idea. Keep them in the same room if you can, so that each will associate the good food with the other. After they eat and groom, they may begin grooming and bonding with the other.

Socialising Your Cat with a Dog

Introducing a new dog to your one-cat home is easier than it is to socialise two cats. Dogs enjoy company since they are pack animals. A dog will become acclimated more easily to kittens as compared to cats.

Introduce the new animal smell, while keeping the dog isolated. Protect the dog when they meet, because cats are more dangerous to dogs, with their lightningfast claws and teeth. Protect your cat, too. Some dogs may see smaller animals as prey. Don't leave the animals together unsupervised until they are fully socialised to each other.

How Do You Socialise a Shy Cat?
If you adopt a kitten or cat who is shy, the process may be traumatising for your new pet. You will need to be very patient when you introduce a new cat into a home where you already have one or more cats. Work with your new cat and reassure the cat already in your home that she is still just as important to you. Socialising a shy cat can take weeks or even months, but it will be time well spent when you can all relax together.

Set Up a Space for Your New Cat

Cats are by nature territorial, but too much territory in the beginning can be a bit overwhelming for your new cat. A small room with no hiding places will work well as a temporary home.

Give your new cat water, food and her own litter box in her special room. You can leave his carrier open and inside the room, with a blanket inside, for a safe spot. Soft music or music on TV may help your new cat to ease into her surroundings, too. Your new cat should remain in her safe room until she is fully socialised with your original cat. If you let her out too soon, she may find a great hiding spot, and set back your Socialisation efforts.

Introducing Yourself

Take this step slowly. Rushing it can set your process back. You will first need your new cat to trust you. Sit with her in her room until she is comfortable coming to you. Move slowly and speak softly. When your new cat is comfortable with you inside her room, you may try holding-out your hand, with the palm facing down.

Let your new cat smell you. If she approaches, hold the hand in position and speak softly to the cat. If she will allow it, stroke the top of her head. Watch her body language with care. If she backs away, you've overstepped the boundaries with which she is comfortable right now. Don't force contact until she is ready for it.

Create Positive Experiences for YourCat

Shy kitty can be bribed into socialising a bit by offering her tasty foods. Treats including deli meat, tuna or wet cat food may be used. Only give her these treats when you sit with her, so she associates one with the other.

In this way, you'll become less fearful and a more positive experience for your shy cat. It may take more than one session for your new cat to eat the treats in your presence. If she doesn't eat them with you in the room, take them with you when you leave the room. She needs to associate the treats with your presence.

Be Patient with Your Shy Cat

Once your new cat is accustomed to yourbeing in the room, she may let you begin to pet her. Proceed with patience until she lets you pet her all over. Move closer as she allows it. When you socialise a cat who is shy, be patient. Whenever your cat is not comfortable, back up to a place where she was comfortable. Move quietly and slowly and remain calm.

Cats progress at different speeds in Socialisation. Some will come more quickly to you, especially if they are young. Others will take more time to learn to trust you.

CHAPTER FOUR
RIGHTING REFLEX
~

Do Cats Always Land on Their Feet?

This question has been asked for centuries, ever since people noticed this uncanny ability of cats to land on their feet even when falling from heights. The Discovery Channel once ran a special program on what is known as the "righting reflex" of cats.

Once you are up more than two or three floors, the cat is able to rotate herself in midair so that she nearly always lands on her feet. Injuries may be sustained, depending on the height from which she falls. Cats have what is termed "nonfatal terminal velocity". This sounds like a simple contradiction, but many smaller animals have this fortuitous advantage. Once she orients herself, a cat can spread out to create an effective parachute. Some cats have fallen 20 or more stories without any injuries. As long as she doesn't land on something that could injure her, she may walk away from the fall.

The Feline Falling Study with an Inherent Flaw

The Journal of the American Veterinary Medical Association brought out a study in 1987, in which two veterinarians examined 132 cats who fell from high windows. These cats were all brought into a New York veterinary hospital, the Animal Medical Center. The average fall for these cats was about five and a half stories, but 90% of these cats survived, even though some had serious injuries. The veterinarians examined the data and discovered that the number of injuries like broken bones increased with the height of the fall, as one would expect. However, this was only true for the cats that fell seven stories or less. Of the cats that fell more than seven stories, the injuries actually declined. The higher the fall, above seven stories, the less chance there seemed to be of serious injury.

The authors of this study explained this result by stating that if a cat falls from more than five stories, she reaches terminal velocity – maximum downward speed – of about 60 mph. After this point, the cats were hypothesized to have spread themselves as you may have seen flying squirrels accomplish. This minimized the injuries. It sounds logical, but there is a fatal flaw in their study, actually mentioned by posters on an unrelated online forum. The flaw? This study was only based oncats brought in for treatment. If your cat fell 20 stories and died, you wouldn't take her to a veterinary clinic. That seems to skew the results of the study, and makes high falls seem safer than they probably are.

The Animal Medical Center's Dr. Michael Garvey was not involved in the original study, but he does not feel that omitting unreported fatalities skews the statistics. He mentioned that the cats that fell from higher heights usually had injuries that suggested they had landed on their chests. This supports the theory that cats can actlike flying squirrels in the air. It was suggested that a cat landing this way had a better chance of surviving than a cat landing in a different position. Dr. Garvey feels that the study is still valid and admits that people may always disagree with any medical study.

How Do Cats Right Themselves?

The ability of cats to fall great distances and land on their feet is usually attributed to their "righting reflex" and to their unique skeleton structure. The "righting reflex" is the ability of a cat to differentiate up and down, then use her natural reflexes to rotate, midair. This orients her body so that her feet will land first. This has been seen in kittens of ages as young as three weeks, and it is believed to be completely developed by the time kittens are eight weeks old. In addition to this righting ability is a flexible backbone in the cat, and her lack of a collarbone. These factors together allow for upper body rotation and flexibility. When a cat turns her forefeet and head, the rest of her body follows and the cat can orient herself and land upright.

"High rise syndrome" is a phrase coined to describe the innate ability of cats to survive falls from great heights and land on their feet. It wasn't until scientists watched flying squirrels and cats in apparent freefall that they noticed both have a low body ratio of volume to weight. They can slow their descent by simply spreading out. Their fluffy coats and relatively low weight allow them to use their high drag coefficient, which gives them a better chance to survive falls.

The Moment of Inertia is Vital

In order for you to understand how a cat can land on her feet when she falls, you have to understand a few concepts related to rotational motion. A cat rotates her body as she falls. The moment of inertia of any object – or any cat – is determined by the distance that its mass is distributed from the axis of rotation. This sounds very scientific, so it may help to picture a ball on a string that you are swinging around your head. The longer the string, the greater the moment of inertia for the ball.

Putting this back into cat terms, if a cat stretches her tail and legs, she can increase her moment of inertia. She can also decrease this moment of inertia if she curls up. The cat can manipulate her moment of inertia by extending and retracting her legs and rotating her tail. This changes the speed of her rotation, giving her control over which body part will contact the ground first. Cats also conserve their angular momentum. When they fall, they change their orientation by reducing their rotational inertia to increase their angular speed. Stretching out their legs increases their rotational inertia and slows their speed. This gives cats the time they need to rotate their bodies so that they will land on their feet.

Just the Facts

Cats need at least three feet of falling distance in order to have the time to right themselves before they land. Cats without tails have the same ability, using their hind legs and conserving momentum to prepare for a landing. The tail is not necessary for this righting reflex to be used. After a cat determines up as opposed to down with her vestibular apparatus, or through visual means, she can twist herself to face down without changing her net momentum. The steps to rotate and safely land have actually been spelled out through observation:

- The cat bends in the middle so the front half of her body rotates on an axis different from the rear of her body. She tucks in her front legs to reduce the inertia moment from the front of her body and extends her rear legs to increase the rear moment of inertia.
- In this way, she can rotate her front half as much as 90 degrees while her rear half is rotated a lot less – as low as 10 degrees – in the opposite direction.
- The cat tucks her rear legs and extends her front legs so that she can rotate her rear body a greater amount than the front of her body.
- Depending on her initial angular momentum and flexibility, the cat may repeat the rotations until she has rotated a full 180 degrees.
- Cats have other features that reduce possible fall damage, in addition to their righting reflex. They are small in size and have a light bone structure. Their fur also decreases the velocity of their falls. Once righted, cats may also spread their body to slow the rate of their descent. As cats reach their terminal velocity of 60 miles per hour (as compared to 130 miles per hour for the average person), they are able to relax, which helps to prevent severe injuries on impact. Some people believe that cats orient their limbs in a horizontal level, so that their body hits the ground before their legs.

CHAPTER FIVE
SCENT SPRAYING & RUBBING
~

You probably love it when your cat comes up and rubs or strokes herself against you with her little chin. Did you know this is part of feline communication?

Scent Glands in Cats

Cats have glands in their lips, forehead, front paws and rear and flank. They secrete pheromones, which act to help your cat to communicate-via chemicals. Cats produce different types of pheromones, which are capable of sending various signals. They also affect your cat's behavior.

Pheromones help your female cat let males know her reproductive status, and they tell them how receptive she will be to them. Pheromones also mark territory and objects, and you. They signal familiarity and comfort. Pheromones in cats are unique – in fact, they are as unique as human fingerprints. Cats deposit them as calling cards, to let everyone know where they have been.

Pheromones that are secreted by the facial glands usually calm your cat. When she rubs her face on objects, she leaves her scent, which is not offensive to people and which is reassuring for your cat. If another cat passes the objects, he or she may stop and smell the scent. If you have a multicat household, other cats may be marking the same objects. Pheromones tell cats who has been in a certain area and when she was there. When you stroke your cat, or when she rubs against your legs, she leaves her benign scent on you, identifying you as her own.

Communicating with Scent

Cats use contact with you or objects in your home to communicate gentle reminders, or urgent needs. Your cat may just be asking for a rub, too. If you have two or more cats, you will probably see that they occasionally rub faces with each other. This is only done if the cats are comfortable in each other's presence.

The act of head rubbing between cats will create a comingling of shared scents that are helpful to cats, since they aid them in feeling more comfortable. They will also mark objects in your home to make themselves more secure in this territory.

Bumping heads is meant to be affectionate. It is something that shows that cats are not always as aloof and independent as we believe them to be. Your cat rubs against you to include you as part of her territory.

Marking Behavior

Communicating by scent is sometimes called "marking behavior". Just as cats use body language, scent is one of their primary methods of communicating with other cats. Using their scents, cats will be able to discern, even from a distance, if a cat now entering their territory is familiar or not. They also mark to leave messages for any other cats in the area.

Outside of urine marking, which is muchdreaded, cats use their scent glands in a more benign way, leaving notice of their presence. Their sense of smell is keen, and some people feel that it may even rival that of dogs. Cats are not trained to search for drugs or bombs, because, unlike dogs, cats will hit on whatever interests them at the time.

Jacobson's Organ

Cats possess a special organ found in the roof of the mouth. It is known as the Jacobson's organ. Cats use it to analyze the chemicals in scents. This specialized organ is useful for any interesting smells, but it is most often used to analyze pheromones. When your cat finds a smell that interests her, she will breathe it in through her mouth. Then it will be "tasted" in the Jacobson's organ. If your cat is using this scent organ, you can tell by looking at her. Her mouth will be open and her lips will curl back a bit. This is known as a
Flehman response. Male horses have the same type of response to mares in heat. Once you see this act once, you will recognize it when you see it again.

Urine Marking

Urine marking is also called spraying, and this is the best-known way utilized by cats to communicate by smell. It is effective for cats, useful in marking territory, exchanging information, announcing their arrival, or threatening another cat. They can disagree with each other without ever coming into physical confrontation. Urine spraying is usually associated with male cats, but females may also spray. Neutering or spaying your cat before he or she reaches sexual maturity will generally stop the spraying behavior even before it starts. It isn't a guarantee, though. Neutered or spayed cats may spray for different reasons than mating. Urine marking is used for conveying other messages, too. Cats who are anxious or stressed may spray. Urine marking is a natural thing for a cat to do. They don't do it out of anger or spite, and they don't know they are being "bad" when they do it. If you punish your cat for spraying, he or she may become upset and and actually spray more often. Modification of the behavior is the proper way to handle urine marking.

Rubbing Is a Communication Tool

You probably hate cat spraying, but you feel very differently when your cat rubs you. Rubbing is part of social communication for your cat. Glands in the face, paw pads and tail release a scent that is unique for each cat. This communicates territory and gives visiting cats information about your cat.

When cats rub against each other as they pass, or rub on your leg, these are behaviors that are social for the cats. Rubbing signals respect and the wish to bond. Rubbing among familiar cats creates a group scent, which increases the familiarity and bonding between all the cats. This is also seen in colonies of feral cats.

Group scent production is believed to have something to do with survival instinct. When a group of cats has a group scent, they know immediately if a cat entering their area is one of their own band or not. When your cat rubs on you, she is including you in her group, and she also adds your scent to the group of cats in your home, if you have more than one cat.

What Is Bunting?

Bunting is a bonding ritual and part of the rubbing techniques that cats use. When your cat bumps her head lightly or rubs it against another cat, or you, it is a bonding behavior. If your cat jumps into your lap, she may bunt against your hand a few times before she settles down to be petted.

When you pet your cat, you are using the human rubbing version. It combines your scent with hers. Allowing your cat to rub you, and petting her, are important aspects of social bonding, and you should look forward to them.

New Cats and Rubbing

With a newer cat, especially if she is an adult, begin your bonding process by simple rubbing. Pet your cat's face and head, as long as she will allow it. You can move gradually onto her flank and then her tail, as she allows it.

When cats who know each other approachin non-hostile situations, they generally greet each other by sniffing nose to nose. Then they progress to rubbing heads or bunting, and sometimes they even lick the other cat's face and ears. As a rule, the more dominant cat will initiate the rubbing.

Dominance among two or more cats does not necessarily mean aggression. Your dominant cat may be quite even-tempered, but he still occupies the top spot in the pecking order. The submissive cat or cats will wait for the dominant cat to begin sniffing or rubbing. If two cats who are not friends encounter each other, there will usually only be a bit of nose to nose sniffing.

When you greet a cat that is not familiar to you, begin by using scent communication. Extend a finger for this cat to sniff. This is a human adaptation of the cat's natural greeting of nose to nose. Don't attempt to pet a cat you don't know. After she sniffs you, if she rubs her mouth or head along your extended finger, she is letting you know that she is comfortable enough and that you may pet her.

If, on the other hand, this new cat backs up and just stares at you, consider this a challenge. Don't try to pet her, or you may be scratched or bitten.

Cat Scratching

In addition to keeping their claws in proper condition, scratching is also a way of communicating through scent, for a cat. The scent glands within the paws leave her unique sent on anything she scratches. She will usually scratch to mark territory. It leaves visual reminders (scratch marks) in addition to scent. Scratching is a natural thing for cats to do, and shouldn't be considered as "bad behavior". Your cat doesn't try to tear up a couch because she is misbehaving or mad. She is doing it to leave her scent and impression. If you don't want your cat scratching your favorite couch or chair, give her other things to scratch.

Scratching posts work very well for most cats. Select a type that won't fall over. Some cats like posts with sisal rope, and others prefer carpeted posts. If you have more than one cat, set up several different areas with cat trees and posts that can be scratched.

The idea here is to give your cat another place to scratch, not to stop her from scratching. It is natural and normal for cats to scratch, and punishing your cat for this will only result in her becoming frustrated or afraid of you.

The Sense of Smell in Cats

Cats have a powerful sense of smell. A cat can easily identify catnip odor, even though its concentration is only one part per billion! When kittens are born, although they are blind and deaf, they can already smell things. Within a day, they will know their home from another nest or house. Each may have her own favorite nipple, too.

Smell is important for cats, since it helps them to recognize friends, enemies and others. If you have multiple cats and take one to the vet, the others may hiss when the vetted cat returns, because of all the new smells on her.

If your indoor cat gets outside, or if you move to a new home with an outside cat, she may become lost if she is more than ten feet from a smell that she knows. She needs to scent her areas, or she won't know how to get home.

If your cat was not socialized when she was a kitten, she may react poorly to changes in her environment, or intrusions of unfamiliar animals, people or objects. Even a new chair may be seen as an invader. Your cat may hide from this interloper. Alternatively, she may rub immediately against it, so that her scent is left there.

Urine Marking and Territory

Once your cat has urinated to mark your home, you must get rid of every bit of the smell. Even if you can no longer smell it after cleaning, your cat might still smell it. A cat's sense of smell is much more powerful than yours.

If you move into a house with a strong odor left by a previous cat occupant, your cat will make sure to mark over these areas. Spend a lot of time socializing your cat when he is still young, and the marking may be less of an issue. Your cat will notice the difference in smell when you board him, take him to his groomer or vet, or even when you bring home a friend who has never been to your house before.

When you move, the transition will be less stressful for your cat if you set up just one room in your new home so that it can be her refuge. Take along something from your old house so that something will be familiar to your cat. Take her to her special room first and let her become acclimated. This works even better for males, since they are much more likely to spray.

If the previous occupants of your new house had a cat, be sure to have the drapes, carpets and any furniture left behind shampooed thoroughly before you bring in your cat.

CHAPTER 6
BODY POSTURE

Cats are not the type of creatures that live in packs, like dogs. Their groupings are looser and not as strictly hierarchical. They will mix with others when they mate, raise kittens or live in groups like multi-cat households or feral colonies.

The posture of cats and its use in body language is subtle and complex, using more than 25 visual signals in 16 unique combinations. There are more nuancesthat are so subtle that humans don't notice them. However, as a cat person, you may learn to recognize some of the body posturing of your cat.

Conveying Messages with Posture

Body posture is most dramatic when rivals are meeting, when territory is in question or during courtship. As a rule, cats will let others pass through their area, but the main area may be protected quite fiercely. Altered cats usually have interactions that are less extreme. Some visual signals may be displayed when cats play, with humans or other cats. Feline body language, including its many postures, is meant to convey messages and to end or avoid physical confrontation.

Both cats want to win their cases without using claws and teeth, since this could injure them both. Cat disputes are often resolved by stare-downs and yelling, rather than by violence. Using subtle body posture, cats may resolve conflicts without humans even knowing that a showdown was in progress. The dominant cat, when he wins a confrontation, walks away from the cat who lost, and sits down. He may groom himself, too.

Look at the Whole Body

Body posture can't be read unless you look at the whole cat body. This includes not only posture, but also the face and the tail position. Looking at just one element may mislead you, since cats combine posture and movements into one message. When a cat arches her back, she is usually upset. However, the same position in a relaxed cat may mean she would like to be rubbed.

Defensive Posture
A cat who feels defensive will erect her fur, so that she appears larger than she is. Dominant cats also attempt the "bigger" look, even accompanied by feline swaggering at times. When cats fluff up like this, they are bluffing, which is used to avoid many types of conflict. Aggressive cats may straighten their legs, making their hind ends higher. The hair along their tail and spine will be erected into a sharp ridge. Defensive cats erect fur ridges, but also puff themselves out.

They will arch their backs and position themselves facing sideways to an aggressive cat. This is another aspect of posture used to make them appear larger than they are. If the aggressive cat pauses, defensive cats may move like crabs in a sideways direction. You may have seen kittensdoing this in mock fights. This is actually a slow retreat used to avoid provoking sudden attacks.

Submissive Posture

Submissive cats want to look unthreatening and small. They may shrink into a crouching position, which indicates that they wish to be left alone. They may even sink onto one side, to demonstrate that they are submissive. If the aggressor still threatens submissive cats, they may roll onto their backs, to appease the dominant cat. Dogs on their bellies are submissive, but cats can still attack from this position. If a submissive cat is in this position and the aggressor jumps on her, she can clasp the aggressor with her forelegs, and the hind legs can scratch at the aggressor. You may have seen this type of behavior when your cat is playing with a toy.

Head Position and Posturing

The position of your cat's head in her overall posture can tell you several things. If she has her head stretched forward, she is trying to see your expression or that of another cat. She may also be encouraging you to interact with her.

If your cat is in conflict, her posture will show a higher head if she is the dominant of the two cats, and the other cat will have her head lowered. When your cat is relaxed, she will usually pull her chin down a bit. Your cat may use her whole body to rub you or a feline friend. The posture here is relaxed and friendly.

Feline Eyes

Humans are very much creatures of eye contact. Your cat does not usually prolong eye contact unless it is to convey assertiveness or when she is threatening another animal. In a room full of people, your cat perceives those looking at her as threatening, which is why she will almost always walk over to someone who isignoring her.

Cats who are rivals may use staring to resolve a conflict. If your cat realizes someone is looking at her, she may assess what she perceives to be a threat, before going on with her previous activity. She may be self-conscious, though. She will become uncomfortable if she is watched studiously.

If you want to reassure your cat after you've been watching her, you can blink slowly. This breaks up your "aggressive" stare and reassures her that you don't mean anything with the stare. Yawning is reassuring, too. Your cat has excellent peripheral vision and doesn't often stare right at something, unless she is getting ready to pounce on a moving object. When your cat daydreams, she does not appear to be looking at anything. However, she is taking in information with her peripheral vision.

The Feline Mouth

Cats do not often use their mouths as a signal of aggression. When your cat opens her mouth to yawn, this is usually interpreted as a non-threat. Open-mouthed hisses or snarls show a cat that is defensive and frightened. Growls are usually done with just a slight opening of the mouth. Sometimes, cats look like they are angry when they are not. If your cat has her ears back and her eyes are narrow slits, it may appear like anger, but she could actually be yawning. Ears may be partly flattened when cats yawn widely.

Cats may sit with their tongues sticking out just a bit. This usually shows relaxation and a sense of contentment. It can be a comical look, but they are usually concentrating. If your cat licks her lips, it may indicate anticipation or anxiety, depending on her surroundings. The fullest use of lip licking is done when catsclean themselves after they eat.

Body Posture and Whiskers

Whiskers are used for judging closed-in areas or object proximity, but this is not their only purpose. They also are indicative of your cat's mood. When your cat is relaxed, her whiskers are relaxed, too, and held slightly off to the side of her head. If she is interested in something, her whiskers may perk forward.

The pads of her cheeks may appear to swell as these muscles pull her whiskers into the position she wants. If your cat is afraid, she may pull her whiskers back alongside her cheeks, in a non-threatening posture.

Feline Ears

The ears of a cat are very mobile. There are 20-30 muscles that control them, so they can move easily up and down and through a 180-degree arc. Sometimes they are flattened backwards or sideways, and sometimes they are pricked forward. Cats can move their ears independently, whether panning around like radar dishes or scanning for nearby sounds. When added to posture, they can communicate effectively. When your cat is relaxed and contented, her ears usually face forward but may tilt back a bit. Even when she is half-asleep, her ears will tell you that she is still alert.

When your cat senses a movement or noise, she will prick her ears and sometimes swivel one or both ears to track the noise source. If your cat becomes anxious, her ears will move back slightly and flatten. Fearful cats have lowered ears. When a cat is fearful but still aggressive, her ears will flatten down sideways. Ears may be used for flagging or flicking, when the ear is moved horizontally as it is flattened. This may be a way cats use to point. Your cat may be deciding between two things, like going to her chair or going outside, when her ears are flagging.

It's All about the Tail

Your cat's tail helps her to balance, and present a confident posture. It also helps her to maneuver at higher speeds. The tail is also a way cats use to communicate. If your cat is hunting – play or for-real – her tail will be almost horizontal behind her. This keeps it from becoming entangled in shrubs.

A twitching tail means that your cat is concentrating and interested in something. This is often the case when your cat is at the window and sees a bird or a squirrel outside. Your cat's tail helps her in communication with you and with other cats. It is quite mobile, with the ability to move up or down and side to side. It may move slowly or thrash like a whip. A curled tail during sleep means your car is very relaxed. A cat who is urine marking will have his tail up and quivering as he treads and dances with his hind feet, in an effort to raise his rear end higher. When your cat greets you, she may extend her tail and quiver it, but this is not related to spraying. It is her way of saying she is very happy to see you. When young cats greet their mother, they will run to her with upright tails. They rub or droop their tails around their rumps to solicit a feeding. Adult cats twine their tails, too. They rub against other cats who are friends and twine their tails together. Most people recognize the so-called bottle brush tail. When a cat has a defensive posture and is threatened, the tail can double in size, as her spinal hair stands erect. It makes her look bigger so that her aggressor will leave her alone.

Posture and Hugging

If you have ever hugged your cat tightly, you may have learned that she doesn't like it. Cats do not like being confined. They prefer simple stroking. Some cats do like hugs, but they are in the minority. If your cat wriggles away when you try to hug her, she is saying, "Thanks, but no thanks."

Relationship Posturing

Cats use their posture to establish or smooth over relationships. If your cat wanders into another cat's territory, she will apologize and use postures to avoid a fight. A confident cat will face unknown things head-on. While using this posture, your cat can defend herself or strike, if necessary. A cat that is fearful turns sideways and arches her back, to get away from the perceived threat. Cats who are surrendering to another cat flatten themselves low to the ground, to appear small. They will tuck in all four

feet and hold their tail and ears tightly against their bodies. Cats who are feeling affectionate may groom you or another cat. They may ask you to play by rolling over and presenting you their tummies. They can also play with you, or cuddle and sleep with you. If your cat sleeps with her back to you, she is showing you the ultimate trust.
Bumping hips and touching noses are signs of affection and trust between cats. If your cat jumps onto your lap and presents you with her backside, this is herequivalent of a handshake. She doesn't mean to offend you by showing you her rear end.

CHAPTER SEVEN
EATING & DRINKING
~

Cats are inherently possessive about the food they eat, and the water they drink. Their ancestors had to fight off others whenever they wanted a meal, and even current day wild or feral relatives of domestic cats don't know where their next meal will come from. Your cat has food available every day, of course, but these habits are deeply ingrained.

Drinking Behavior

It is vital for a cat, like any animal, to drink healthy amounts of water each day. Water doesn't seem like a nutrient, but it does account for two-thirds of your cat's body weight. It is the basis for all of the chemical processes in her body. Water transports all your cat's necessary oxygen and nutrients through her body. Water carries these essentials through the cat's bloodstream and into her cells. It moisturizes air located in her lungs an regulates her body temperature.

Water transports all your cat's necessary oxygen and nutrients through her body. Water carries these essentials through the cat's bloodstream and into her cells. It moisturizes air located in her lungs and regulates her body temperature. Water is also essential in the elimination of waste products after your cat metabolizes everything she needs from her food and drink.

Cats Fed Wet Food Don't Need a Lot of Water

Your cat's water requirements are based almost totally on her food's moisture content. Wild cats get most of the water they need from prey that has been freshly killed. Your cat can go for a long time without water, as long as her canned food contains a high moisture percentage. If the moisture level in her food drops below 61%, she will need extra water. You probably already have a water bowl for her, right beside her food bowl. Even your domestic cat has a thirst drive, and she will guard her food, since that is where she is accustomed to getting the fluid she needs. Her ancestors and wild relatives will fight to the death to defend their prey. Even if she is dehydrated, though, your domestic cat will not initiate drinking as dogs do.

Guarding Food

Cats may do well on dry foods, but canned foods are healthier in many ways for her. Your cat probably wouldn't care as much if your dog sneaks in and steals some of her dry food, but she will react much more violently if the dog tries to take hercanned food.

Your domestic cat may even react to your dog's attempt to make off with her dry food. It is so ingrained in her psyche to guard her food that she may protect even food she is not intent on eating in the next few days. A cat's urinary tract is much healthier if it has the appropriate amount of fluid within it. Cats are all carnivores, despite what some cat food manufacturers might tell you. They count on their meat to get the fluids their body needs. Cats are inherently able to get most of their water requirements through their kill. Therefore, it is most understandable then, that your domestic cat protects her food so fiercely. It is hard wired into her psyche.

CHAPTER EIGHT
KNEADING

One of the most appealing habits of cats, as far as humans are concerned, is kneading their paws. It is also called "making biscuits", because it does look as though cats are kneading bread dough when they do it.

What Is Kneading?

When your cat kneads, she rhythmically alternates her paws, pushing against soft objects or your lap. Some cats don't use their claws when they knead, while others do. Some cats even knead with all four paws.

There are cats that do not knead, but it is very common for young and old cats. Why do cats knead? There are various ideas about this topic, as there are about many aspects of cat behavior.

Some cats purr and knead when you pet them, but they might also do it while sitting alone on your bed, for no apparent reason. Cats start kneading when they are young. When kittens nurse, they knead to stimulate the flow of milk in their mother's nipples. However, no one knows exactly why they carry this habit beyond the nursing age.

Your Cat May Knead You

Your cat may enjoy kneading in your lap while she is being petted. Unfortunately, if she uses her claws in this action, it can be painful for you. You may try to pet her on the belly instead, but not all cats are fond of that. You will not want to punish your cat if she hurts you while she is kneading. She does not realize that you are hurting. If you use nail guards or keep her nails trimmed, it can be easier on you when she kneads.

Stretching

Cats have their own type of yoga, and it works out their muscle kinks just as stretching does for you. Kneading is a way cats can keep their muscles limber. Your cat's feral ancestors preferred sleeping on soft surfaces. They would often knead leaves or tall grasses to make a bed – or a nest, if a mother lion or tiger was having cubs. Kneading also allows cats to be sure there are not unwelcome rodents lying in the foliage.

Kneading for Territorial Reasons

Cats are very territorial, and kneading with their paws leaves their scent on their belongings. This includes you, too. Cats activate the scent glands in the pads of their paws to mark things or people by kneading. Female cats sometimes knead their paws before they go into heat. This is a display for male cats that they are available and ready to mate.

Kneading Is Instinctive

Kneading is instinctive, even after a cat is no longer nursing from her mother. Adult cats who knead may be doing it to:

- Calm themselves when stressed
- Show contentment
- Mark their human with their scent
- Mark objects with their scent
- One old theory said that adult cats who kneaded were taken away from their mothers at too early an age. This was debunked long ago, since almost all cats knead. It seems to be quite simply something that comforts them, whether they are happy or stressed.
- Kneading may become obsessive for some adult cats. They may even suckle on clothing, blankets or stuffed toys while they knead.

CHAPTER NINE
FELINE INTELLIGENCE

Dog and cat owners enjoy bragging about the intelligence level of their favorite pets. There is a long debate about whether cats are smarter than dogs. Not surprisingly, the owners of each type of pet feel that their pet is smarter.

The Dog versus Cat Intelligence Debate

Dog owners point to the fact that their pets can perform tricks. Cat owners feel that their pets are simply too intelligent to perform tricks on command. The question isn't as easy as that, though – it's the animal equivalent of comparing apples and oranges. Dogs are primarily pack animals, and they need to follow their top dog, which in domestic settings is their owner. Cats are more solitary and do not answer to anyone. Their only motivation is survival.

While cats don't often perform tricks, they are certainly adaptable and clever, in their own way. Cats are self-reliant and resourceful, and have lived for thousands of years in many diverse environments. Even your domestic cat shows a versatile, strong-willed and crafty nature.

Mastering Cat Language

Your cat's remarkable physical and mental abilities are often thought of as simply instinctive. However, they taketime to master their language and hone the abilities with which they are born. Cats do not learn in the same way as dogs. They have their own unique type of intelligence.

Cats Don't Forget

Once your cat attains knowledge, whether through trial and error or accident, that knowledge will be retained for her whole life. She has an excellent memory. Techniques in hunting, even while largely unused, can be easily recalled if your cat ever wanders off and has to fend for herself.

Cats are easily frightened, so they retain strong memories of incidents that they consider threatening. They also store and recall happy experiences, especially those related to play or food. Domestic cats respond very well to sounds that are familiar to them, like the opening of a can of cat food. Many cats also know when it's mealtime, even if there is no other way to know in addition to hunger and an internal clock of some sort.

Tricks and Training

As the psyche of cats has become more understood, felines have been trained for performance in films and TV series. They don't perform for a pat on the head, but they can be trained with food. Cats learn especially well if their owner is the trainer and if play or food is involved as a reward. The owners of cats claim that their pets are simply too smart to do the types of tricks that you have seen dogs do. Other people are naysayers when it comes to the subject of feline intelligence, since they won't do tricks as easily as dogs will.

Assessing Feline Intelligence

Testing animal intelligence is not always humane. Researchers used to insertelectrodes into a cat's brain to stimulate behaviors or to monitor the cat's brain activity. Subjects have been killed by inhumane testing. More recently, tests have been performed in settings more natural for domestic cats. Tests should take into account the innate behavior of animals, as well as their instincts. In tests where dogs and cats were navigating mazes, cats did not perform well, as far as humans were concerned. Dogs learned their way through the maze to reach a reward. Cats relaxed and looked into blind alleys and took baths. Cats are not as motivated to seek treats as dogs are. The blind alley investigations made sense for cats, because who knew what prey there might be inside them?

Dogs are more likely to cooperate in tests that show how eager they are to please their masters. Dogs have also been bred over the years to reduce some traits and to enhance ease of training. Cats have different social structures. Male cats often wander, looking for females, rather than remaining in a group. When large food sources are found, they may form loose colonies. However, the social structure is closer to that of a pride of lions than to a pack of dogs.

Cooperating with humans, for cats, is only limited, unless the cats' interests are served when they perform tasks. Dogs have been bred for many years to make them more useful for people. Cats are mainly bred for appearance. This doesn't mean that they are less intelligent; it simply means that they don't need to do tricks to get what they need.

Response to Stimuli

Early psychologists felt that all types of behavior were the result of stimulus and response. Their first theories did not leave room for innate behaviors, instinct,consciousness, thinking or predispositions to specific behaviors.

Learning, when reduced to its simplest level, means associating stimuli that were previously unrelated. Learning also involves the assessment of actions and their consequences. Present experiments are geared to provide a more complete knowledge of the psychology of felines. Electrodes placed in the brains of cats don't always tell scientists what they need to know, other than the fact that cats mainly react to hunger, thirst and other vital stimuli.

Is Learning just Simple Association?

Psychologists in the past believed that all learning was simply association. The response to stimuli was even considered to be true in the case of humans, too. Today, it is understood that many breeds of mammals have mental processes that are more complex. Many higher animals have their own representation of the world they live in, and how it works. They consult this world when they make decisions. It will never be completely possible to understand the way cats perceive or understand their world. Virtual reality gives us some idea of how the world sounds and looks like for cats. In order to fully investigate the intelligence of felines, and their ability to learn, more humane testing is needed, and this testing must be better suited for cats. In order for this to happen, researchers need to know how today's cats have evolved in a way that suits their lifestyle and environment. There will always be some things that predispose cats to behave in specific ways.

Cats in Their Natural Environment

In the natural environment of a cat, an unconditioned stimulus may be something as simple as pain that was inflicted by a tomcat. The response to this unconditioned stimulus may involve flight, in order to avoid further pain. After one experience, the sight of an aggressive tomcat (which is now considered conditioned stimulus) may cause flight. This is a conditioned response, since the cat's motivation is avoiding pain. Conditioned learning can be more complicated, when you consider your cat's innate behaviors. Her ears hone in on noises, so experiments may utilize sounds, followed by food. However, testing isn't that easy. Actual research has shown that, instead of running for the food, cats searched the area of the loudspeaker over which the sound was broadcast. This does not mean that cats are dumb. To the cats, the sound indicated prey, so they went directly to the source of the sound.

What Is Intelligence?

Humans bias their studies by assessing other species' intelligence by relating it to our own. Animals with dexterous hands and good eyesight are rated highly. However, cats cannot react to stimuli by using their "hands". Cats are not less intelligent because they do not respond like monkeys in certain tests. They may be less cooperative, but that doesn't make them dumb. Animals like cats that rely on instinct can readapt only at a pace that is determined by mechanisms in their evolution. Cats can actually solve problems outside their adaptations to their niche in the environment. These abilities allow cats to cope with unexpected changes, but they are difficult to measure. A domestic cat, left to her own devices, will take on some of the behaviors of feral cats, once she realizes that she is on her own. Her kittens may be born feral, but if they are adopted back into the human world, they will revert to the behavior of domestic cats, as long as they are socialized when they are very young.

IQ and Cats

Humans quite often define animal intelligence in the terms of "IQ". There are various scoring systems used in IQ tests, and you can learn how to perform them better. Some very intelligent people don't do well on standard IQ tests because those tests are biased to logical reasoning, or are skewed, culturally. Cats and dogs don't need to understand the same things you do, in order to survive. The intelligence of animals islinked to their natural environment and their basic survival needs. Humans must adapt their perception of what intelligence is, and formulate tests that are appropriate for the animals they are studying. Different types of animals have very different innate behaviors. If let loose into a group of baby ducks, a dog may try to herd them, while a cat may try to attack them, in search of food. This doesn't mean that either animal is less intelligent. Each animal performed based on his or her innate instincts.

CHAPTER TEN
HUMAN BEHAVIOUR INFLUENCES

Often how we behave with and around our cats will determine how they behave. Many of us don't even realise how we are influencing certain behaviour in our feline friends.

Non-Cat Lovers and Cat Attention

Cats like to go for the one person in the room who doesn't like cats. Why? If a cat walks in and is greeted with many people talking at him all at the same time, using body language that suggests "come here, we want to touch you", he might feel overwhelmed or threatened and seek solace from the calmer person who is just sitting there, saying nothing, doing nothing, remaining still and avoiding interaction. By this we can tell cats read us like books to such an extent that what we do shapes what they do.

The "Meow" Just For Humans

The number one thing humans like to do with their cats is talk to them. In fact, probably almost every cat owner talks to their cat, whether it's to comfort them, tell them off, greet them, express affection and so on. What various cat behaviourists and experts have recently discovered is that cats have tapped into this. Cats have noticed that when they meow we often respond to them, so cats have established this vocalisation to communicate with us and get what they want. In fact, cats are known only to meow to people and not to other cats. This is a sure sign they behave according to how we behave towards them.

Obeying Some and Ignoring Others

Cat experts have even discovered that cats, even within the home, still have a hierarchy in mind. The tone, communication and body language of one human in the home may cause them to react with obedience. But someone who takes a relaxed approach to the cat's behaviour, e.g. never telling her to "get down" from the kitchen sink when others do, will get different reactions from their cat. That's why if someone who never tells her cat to get down from the kitchen sink and suddenly decides to, the cat is likely to ignore her. It just goes to show how cats behave according to each individual human's nature and personalities.

Why Punishment Defeats the Point

Cats don't associate punishment from a human to something they (the cat) did. They purely react to the negative reaction from their owner and become confused and scared. Regular punishment just encourages the cat to avoid people because cats are responsive towards your behaviour and don't necessarily know why you do it. They will fear that you will do it again. So, though some people think shouting or causing physical harm prevents them from behaving in a particular way, it actually causes the relationship to break down and the problem they are being punished over will get worse instead of better. They do not perceive things in the same way as we do and will do something by encouragement as opposed to punishment. Positive reinforcement gets behaviour done the way you desire because cats are likely to repeat the good behaviour when a reward is due at the end of it.

The Cat and the Baby

Those with babies or toddlers may have noticed their cat's behaviour change when the baby is present. Firstly, cats will behave differently to any changes in the home, including new family members and the change of routine may cause stress. The cat may also not be familiar with babies and be unsure of what they are and what they could do. This is why so many cats avoid babies or retreat or curl up in defence when experiencing one. When something or someone comes along and suddenly gets a lot more attention than your cat, your cat will notice. You may see them attempt to get your attention when 'jealousy' occurs. Having a baby turns the house upside down – rooms are closed off, new objects and furniture are everywhere, new sounds and smells are experienced… The cat won't be wonderfully happy about this. Some cats have enough of it and leave for long periods of time. The best solution is to try and keep your cat's routine the same as possible and, though difficult with a baby, spend time giving your cat the atten tion they need.

The Cat When You're at Home

Your cat will behave differently when you're at home. When you're away they get up to whatever they want. More clingy cats may have a hard time being alone and suffer from separation anxiety. This undesired behaviour spans from not having you around and becoming depressed or anxious being alone and unstimulated.

When you are home, however, lots of cat's attention will change drastically from whatever they were doing to the human. Cats run to doors when people enter the house, just like dogs, and this is particularly common in lone indoor cats. They also do this to greet you.

Once you're in the same space your cat will, at least half the time, want to communicate with you by meowing and creating signals according to what they want. Domesticated cats are more adapted to knowing and getting what they want from humans, so they behave accordingly. Your cat may sit or paw at the toys to suggest wanting to be played with, or run out near the food bowl, meow at you and rub their face against your legs.

Cats are more intelligent than we think, particularly around their human owners. Claims cats are "manipulative" aren't far wrong. Cats learn exactly how they can get things from us and what kind of behaviour they need to exhibit to get it. This is why training is almost always needed with cats, right from when they are kittens. But we are all still victims of a cat's intelligence. They are so clever and so subtle in what they do that sometimes we barely notice their behavioural impact on us and our behavioural impact on them. Whoever says cats are mysterious creatures are actually very right indeed.

CHAPTER ELEVEN
INDOOR AND OUTDOOR CATS

Outdoor cats are pets we allow to go outdoors into the garden and the neighbourhood to explore and the majority of cat owners allow this. Indoor cats are pets we keep indoors permanently and this small percentage, about 10% in the UK, is beginning to grow. Why is this?

People decide on having an indoor cat for a variety of reasons: owners could be living in an apartment or flat or anywhere like this where there is no garden, owners could be living in a densely populated and busy area with main roads making the outside world high risk for their cat, the cat could be a specific pedigree breed that cost a lot of money and would risk being stolen if allowed outside, the cat could have a medical condition which limits its senses or mobility and therefore makes going outside dangerous, the cat could be unsprayed and risk unwanted breeding, or owners fear their cat will get killed or lost.

Needs and Behaviours

Some even believe their cat could be safer ad healthier having an indoor lifestyle, but does an indoor cat's behaviour and needs differ from outdoor ones?

The answer is yes. There are upsides and downsides to an indoor cat's behaviour, but there are also upsides and downsides to an outdoor cat's behaviour, too. This is purely because their environments are so wildly different that their needs also differ. An environment shapes the way a cat behaves. Indoor cats are safer and healthier in an indoor environment because they are not exposed to dangers that outdoor cats are at risk from such as passing cars, other territorial cats and animals, parasites, hazards such as pesticides and infectious diseases. They also have a very low risk of getting lost, a potentially heart-breaking problem which leads to the dreaded "lost cat" posters found on lampposts.

The fact that people are keeping their cat indoors because they are conscientious and want to protect them is great, but there is a growing argument about whether people are infringing on a cat's natural desire to explore and hunt. When we look at how long cats have been domesticated compared to how long animals have existed, we can see they've actually only been domesticated for a short period of time and, of course, they still possess these predatory instincts – their ancestors, after all, are large, menacing hunters who roam the wild roaring and chasing prey.

Indoors cats, however, can become very unstimulated, bored, frustrated and even develop problems such as depression, anxiety, compulsive disorders, aggression, clinginess and various other behavioural issues. This is normally down to being denied the activities they have deep-rooted within their instincts – climbing, jumping, running, pouncing, clawing, chewing, stalking and so on. The outside holds mystery: trees to climb, plants to hide in, small animals to prey on and lots of exciting things to witness and explore to stimulate their minds and bodies. Cats are territorial, however, and any one neighbourhood is bound to have multiple cats roaming it. This means cats are likely to fight and many cats will suffer stressed outdoor lives.

The very natural fact regarding a cat's instincts and needs causes a confliction regarding the best interests of your cat. Can we allow our cats to be healthy and safe away from the dangers of the big, wide world while ensuring they are being stimulated and are given the chance to explore their instincts?

You're much less likely to get unusual behaviour from your indoor cat if you try and recreate the outside world in your house. By this we don't mean plant trees and let loose some wild rodents! We mean you should try and use alternative things and activities that stimulate your cat just as the outside world would.

Outdoor cats scratch just about anywhere that feels a good texture for their claws e.g. the bark from a tree. Your indoor cat may need a few scratching posts or scratching surfaces they can perform their necessary clawing and stretching on. Not just claws, but their teeth will also require objects to chew on – chew treats are good, but shouldn't be given all the time. Try buying cat toys with different, chewable textures to them.

The hunting activities can be played out by engaging with your cat with various predator-related games: pull around a toy mouse on a string to encourage pouncing and chasing, throw bouncy balls up to be jumped at, wiggle a toy on a cat tree perch so your cat climbs up to get it, move a toy attached to a stick or string along the floor from a distance to encourage stalking, etc. If you engage your cat with this at least twice a day you will find they are much happier and more stimulated, not to mention they are being kept active and will maintain a healthy weight as a result. Just be careful not to attract your cat to your hands or feet otherwise you'll be unintentionally encouraging them to attack you.

The behaviour of an outdoor cat may be slightly different since they are being more stimulated away from home. This doesn't mean you shouldn't play with them, however. Playing with your cat will keep them happy, fit and maintain a good relationship with you.

Outdoor cats may display 'wilder' behaviour by bringing home their

They may also shows signs they have been in a fight as they will have a whole neighbourhood of cats to contend with. Your cat will have picked up the scents of other felines and outlined exactly which territory is considered 'theirs' and where exactly they are going over this 'border' into another cat's territory. This is why cats tend to always walk along the same routes as they know from experience where is safe and where is a no-go zone.

Cats may come home behaving anxiously or behave in the garden or home timidly and highly observant. This is normally because they have had bad experiences with neighbouring cats where territorial behaviour has been displayed. Some cats may be very distressed, but this can also be said for indoor cats. Indoor cats with major changes occurring in their homes may wish to escape to the outside. Some even do so for several hours or even several days. This is why it is important to create a balance that has the cat's welfare at heart.

Though there is a case for both sides of the debate, it's down to you as a cat owner as to whether you have an outdoor or indoor cat. Normally it's easier to have an indoor cat from the very beginning as going from outdoors to indoors can be very difficult and frustrating for the cat and yourself. Quite a few veterinary professionals opt for the indoor cat option purely because of all the possible dangers outweighing the upsides. They do, however, only recommend an indoor cat on the condition that owners compensate for what the cat is missing out on from the outdoors. They rely heavily on their home and their owners, so keep a safe home with all the enrichment a cat could need as well as plenty of regular attention from yourself and other family members. You could even consider getting another cat for their company.

CHAPTER TWELVE
ADOLESCENT AND SENIOR CATS

Your cat's behaviour will change and differ from kittenhood, adolescence and when they are much older. It's important to understand the common behaviours associated with each so you know what to expect at each stage in your beloved feline's life.

Adolescent Behaviour

Earlier in this book you would have explored the importance of introduction of new things and socialisation for kittens and how it shapes their behaviour. But what is the behaviour like when they grow out of being a newbie kitten and become an 'adolescent'?
When humans become teenagers lots of things change – this is the same for a cat. Between the ages of 6 and 12 months your cat is experiencing their adolescent period. They may start to gain confidence in doing things after spending time growing accustomed to their environment. Some say that at around 12 months, the cat is the equivalent of 15 years old in human age.

During the teenage period your cat will reach sexual maturity. After around 6 months they are able to have kittens of their own and females will start to come into season. Signs your cat has started going into season include increased vocalisation (calling), more affection towards owners, floor rolling, tail flicked to one side, front body on the ground while rear pointed upwards, licking of genitals, rubbing against people and objects with face, hind feet treading and increased need to go outside. This typically lasts between one week and 10 days and the 'mating season' is more likely from spring to autumn. Once finished it is likely to re-occur every 14 to 21 days unless she becomes pregnant or is spayed (neutered).

Going into season can cause tricky and unwanted behaviour and consequences, so it's always advised to get your cat spayed unless you intend to breed her. Once spayed, she will not go into season and display these typical behaviours.

Males also experience puberty around 6 months of age. This is when typical behaviour such as roaming and urine marking will occur. Experts also say unsprayed male cats will be more aggressive than spayed ones, so it is strongly advised to get yours spayed unless you intend to breed from him.

Common trouble behaviour will be prevented through spaying, but in order to do it at exactly the right time you must speak with your vet and they will do what is necessary when the time is right.

Behaviour in Senior Cats

Behaviour can change with age, particularly when the cat reaches the later stages of life and aging begins to occur. Cats are expected to live until 12 years of age, but it's not uncommon to see cats live much longer than this.

Common behavioural changes in an aging cat include more vocalisation – though this could be mistaken for a cat being very sociable or having problems with stress or anxiety, it could also have an age-related cause. It could be from disorientation, a side effect of a feline cognitive decline or FCD that can occur in old age. It could alternatively be from the health woes of old age, such as medical conditions like arthritis or deafness. Always check this out with your vet.

Old cats commonly experience increased likelihood of waking up during the night and general restlessness. As with humans, age can cause a decline in the senses for cats – vision and hearing will not be as good as it used to be and this could affect the cat's sleeping habits. They will also need to eliminate more, but getting to the litter tray may prove difficult if they suffer from feline cognitive decline. Anxiety can also increase with age, particularly at these quiet night times where you are asleep – being apart from you or not being able to navigate around the home could make this anxiety worse.

It's heart-breaking to have an elderly relative with Alzheimer's disease, but it can also be sad to have a cat who suffers from a lot of the same symptoms of the human disease. Elderly cats can become very confused and forgetful of what used to be well-known and comforting to them – this is why vets recommend cats are given familiar routines and samey environments that don't change, as not only do they naturally love routine, but older cats with confused and forgetful symptoms can live a little easier.

Lots of owners of senior cats report problems with elimination around the house. The cat can start to eliminate outside of their litter tray and this can be down to poorer mobility from old age and age-related conditions, age-related incontinence or a health problem for which they have a higher susceptibility due to their older age. Easy access litter trays and more of them in the house will help this matter, but always get your cat checked at the vets to rule out any serious problems and find suitable management for those problems.

Older cats are known to either distance themselves more from their owners or do the opposite and become increasingly clingy around humans for constant contact. Drastic changes to personality and behaviour like this can be confusing, but always remain a caring and loving owner giving your cat everything they need from balanced diet and exercise, to affection, play time and regular vet check-ups.
Age impacts the body. Things wear down and problems can occur such as a lesser mobility, arthritis or other illnesses. A decreased level of activity is common in old cats who are naturally slowing down. Ensure to encourage your cat to keep active according to their abilities and at their pace, as well as grooming them regularly in times where they may not groom themselves. If energy levels really taper off and your cat stops doing the necessities, such as eating, you must contact your vet right away.

An old cat who is stiff, slow, weaker, less agile and mobile, who has decreased senses may become more irritated quickly. Having age-related physical limitations can have a mental impact that could cause depressed, lethargic, irritated, sad and confused cats. Be sure to give your cat space if they are irritated and try and keep the cat included in social activities unless they show signs of disinterest.

Poor vision, hearing and sense of smell from age means cats are less likely to be aware of people, animals and their environment. This could mean they become defensive or scared more easily and this could lead to aggression. Be sure to be calm and gentle around your cat. If the problem gets worse your vet will need to check over your cat and medications may be prescribed to ease the behaviour.

Unusual behaviour is more likely in older senile cats, cats with feline cognitive decline or cats affected by age-related illnesses. It may cause unusual actions such as repetitive or compulsive pacing. Any physical or mental behavioural changes need to be addressed by a vet just to rule out any serious issues and diagnose the exact problem so possible solutions are found for a more comfortable and easier life.

CHAPTER THIRTEEN
DEALING WITH DIFFICULT BEHAVIOUR

It's unrealistic to expect our cats to be wonderfully behaved all the time. As conscientious cat owners it's important to recognise when a cat's behaviour becomes unacceptable. It is only then when we can take the steps to alter the behaviour for the better.

Though there is a lesser focus on dealing with undesirable behaviour from cats compared to dogs, it is still a necessary issue to address. The word "training" should not be exclusively used when talking about dogs because cats can be trained to behave well and to kick bad habits.

Behaviour in a Multi-Pet Household

Having more than one cat can be problem-free with the cats getting along harmoniously, but for some it's incredibly difficult and full of tension. With cats that have spent their lives together since they were kittens, it's more likely they will get along than not. Cats who are together in the same 'social group' will happily engage in sleeping near each other, grooming each other and playing with each other.

However, as with humans, cats can be incompatible socially with each other and this makes home life a stressful time. Cats that are split into different 'social groups' will hiss at each other, fight, vocalise aggressively, occupy different areas of the home, change their posture around each other, be more vigilant, engage with humans at different times and restrict behaviours with other cats around them. This often makes feeding times and other communal activities hard because most owners feed their cats in one area of the house and put litter trays in one area, too.

Having to live in the same house with other socially incompatible cats is a stressful and anxious experience for your felines, with this stress leading to further unwanted behaviours such as communicative and territorial urine marking, hiding away for long periods, or retreating to specific 'safe places' – even ones away from the home or in other houses.

Other reasons for aggression and tension between cats at home could be maternal instinct – a protective mother keeping other cats that are not part of the litter away, but this behaviour will ease off when the kittens are weaned. Other aggression between cats is seen during rough play sessions, but this is normally just pretend play to act out the activities of a hunter - stalking, pouncing, ambushing, biting and so on. Usually injury is unlikely and cats learn if they've gone too far when the other cat reacts.

Spaying is often suggested to be a good solution for both female and male cats. Female cats will benefit from spaying because it will stop her going into season as well as prevent any further maternal aggression occurring. Males are known to become less aggressive after being neutered, too. Always break up any fighting with a noise, clap or firm command. If fighting occurs regularly you could separate the cats for a 'time out' session to calm things down. As mentioned previously, communal food bowls and litter trays don't help – if two cats are fighting create two separate eating and litter areas so they can eat and eliminate without anxiety. Give an aggressive cat space, but always reward them when they are behaving well. If temporary separation doesn't work, try doing it for longer periods and adopt the upstairs and downstairs cat plan. Re-introduce the cats later on gradually and never force a meeting for reconciliation. Small manageable chunks are best and quickly separate them if tensions heighten.

Sometimes behavioural issues between cats are so problematic they require veterinary attention, with referrals to behaviourists or even behavioural medication prescribed. In extreme cases, rehoming may be the best option, particularly if the cat's quality of life is being downgraded from the stress. Households with several cats are more likely to have compatibility issues, so rehoming is often the best solution.

Cats With Fears, Stress and Anxiety

Cats with fears, stress or anxiety cannot be helped unless the causes behind it are found. But firstly, you need to notice the signs your cat will display.

Generally, an anxious or stressed out cat may display signs such as hair loss, loss of appetite, spraying or eliminating in the house, repetitive movement, trembling, excessive vocalisation, hiding and being reluctant to socialise or play, or more serious signs of illness that causes your cat to become distressed.

A cat with separation anxiety will behave differently when you leave the house. They could become destructive, vocal, urinate inside the house and other unwanted behaviours. If you experience anything like this when you leave or once you're back, then your cat could be suffering from separation anxiety. You will need to leave your cat lots of puzzle toys and things to do while you're gone. Even the presence of another person or pet may help. Never make a big deal out of leaving or returning as this could teach your cat to make a big deal out of it too. Ease your cat into coping alone by leaving them for short periods of time and increasing the length of absence once you notice your cat tolerating it better.

Changes to the environment is a common reason for a scared and stressed feline – moving house, travelling, new people or pets in the house, taking them to a cat show, or even what we would perceive as insignificant changes such as buying new furniture. Cats love routine and being familiar with their space, but when this is suddenly and drastically changed the unknown will scare them. If change is inevitable, try to do it gradually at a pace your cat can handle. It's important to keep your cat surrounded by the things it loves and knows well, such as favourite toys.

Sometimes stressful situations cannot be avoided and we must focus on changing the response of the cat to these situations. Comforting and distracting your feline will help, but there are two methods you can try to ease anxiety and fear in cats. Though these two methods are often used with dogs, you can still adopt the same techniques. There are as followings:

The De-sensitisation Method

De-sensitisation is about exposing the fear at a very small and manage able level. A cat scared of loud noises could be played similar sounds on the radio at low volume. Once they have adapted to this noise level and realised everything is fine, you can turn the volume up and keep doing so step-by-step according to how your cat copes.

A cat afraid of human or animal visitors in the home may be exposed to them at a distance to begin with, with gradual closeness and interaction occurring when the cat learns to adapt to each level properly. Patience and keeping to your cat's pace will help enormously.

The Counterconditioning Method

Counterconditioning is used along with de-sensitisation and this method is all about re-teaching your cat how to react in the stressful situation. The panic, retreat, fright and anxiety felt when experiencing loud noises or visitors can be replaced with feelings of happiness, fun, excitement and affection by giving your cat pleasant things to experience when it is happening. Give them attention, play games, give them brand new toys, give them some new treats, give them their favourite massage – anything you know they enjoy should be given every time the feared situation arises. Hopefully your feline will learn to associate the situation with pleasure instead of fear.

If all else fails or if you're unsure of why your cat is anxious or stressed you could benefit by having a consultation with your vet. Remember an anxious and stressed cat is not a happy one. The vet may have some good tips or could refer your cat to a behaviourist. Seeing your vet is particularly advised if the anxiety doesn't appear to go away and your cat has other worrying symptoms and behaviour.

Aggressive Behaviour Towards Humans

Trust can diminish when your cat tries their luck and shows aggression towards you, visitors or even children. Forming a good relationship with your feline will then prove tricky. We need to understand why our cat becomes aggressive towards us and what we can do to stop this before having a pet becomes a hindrance rather than a pleasure.

Earlier in the book you would have become familiar with the body language and vocalisation of a cat according to its mood. If you're more aware of this you will be able to predict when your cat is about to become aggressive. Watch out for a cat attempting to look more intimidating or a cat becoming defensive, as these are the two forms of aggression:

Signs of Offensive Aggression

Look out for a stiff posture, with stiff legs and tail. Your cat's face will consist of an unswerving stare, a change in the size of his pupils and pricked up ears moved slightly forward. Their rear will be raised up and their fur may raise upwards along their back and tail. If they are vocal you're likely to hear a growl or howl. He will have no problems facing you directly.

Signs of Defensive Aggression

The cat's head will tuck inwards and he will be in stooped position. The tail will be hidden away or curled around the body. His face will consist of dilated pupils, his whiskers will draw inwards, his mouth may be open to vocalise a hiss and his ears will be flattened. His fur will also raise and, unlike an offensive cat, he is more likely to face you indirectly.

Both signs of aggression could include physical attacks such as biting, taking a swipe with their paws, clawing, growling, grabbing and exposing teeth and claws.

When you notice this behaviour you need to remember the situation . Does it always happen during a specific interaction or activity? Do you scare or anger your cat because of a specific action? Cats can become aggressive for various reasons listed below:

Redirected Aggression

A cat provoked by someone or something he cannot access may unleash the aggression on someone nearby whom he can access. The aggression prompter could be anything from observing other cats outdoors, stalking prey, having a bad experience with another animal, hearing uncomfortable or startling noises, animal scents and sounds, an indoor cat returning home after escaping outdoors, a human interrupting a cat-on-cat fight and so on.

Redirected aggression is not something the cat purposely seeks out to do, but more likely an almost automatic behaviour when someone bothers a distressed cat or happens to be close by. This is usually the reason behind people claiming their cat attacks them very randomly for no apparent reason. The solution is to leave an agitated cat alone for a few hours and giving them the space they need to calm down.

Play Time Aggression

Rough play is normal. It involves all the natural predatory processes felines get up to and it's natural for your cat to pounce around and act out hunting behaviour during play. As rough play is prevalent in cats playing with other cats, this could also be present in play with humans. It is particularly known in younger cats and they should learn how to control the roughness to which they play from a young age. Reasons behind aggressive play involve cats that are left lone for long periods of time with no chances to play, cats who haven't been able to learn when young to inhibit painful aggression, and cats with owners who actively encourage them to ambush people during play time activities.

Leaving your cat for long periods of time unstimulated will drive them crazy – especially with indoor cats. Try and play with them as often as you can, at least twice a day, and involve new and exciting toys of different varieties – mice on strings, wind-up toys, puzzles with treats inside, bouncy or Ping-Pong balls, chew toys, etc. Even boxes and similar items are great ways for cats to explore and have fun. Toys are also a great way to distract a cat as soon as they show aggression. Aside from regular play and plenty of toys, you have to show your cat when enough is enough. When he bites or scratches you it's time to stop the activity and walk away, giving your cat some time to calm down. It's all about saying "fun time is over if you attack me."

Physical intervention or dangling hands or feet in your cat's way will provoke further aggression, as will physical punishment.

Aggression Out of Fear

Something or someone may scare your cat and make them feel insecure and threatened. A cat may switch to defensive mode and, with a lack of places to escape to, he could lash out as a means of protecting himself. Always remember to recognise a specific fear and do everything possible to stop it from happening, or at least train your cat to cope with it better. In this particular instance with a cat attacking as a defensive reaction, you must leave him alone and give him a chance to relax.

Aggression from Pain and Frustration

A cat that is ill or in pain will not always appreciate being bothered by their owners. A cat being hurt will lash out, as will a cat in pain being handled which in turn causes more pain. Cats in pain may also become aggressive if they predict a human close by may wish to touch them. This is often why punishing a cat physically makes aggression a lot worse.

If you suspect your cat is not well or in pain, then aggression is a sure sign they are not happy. An underlying medical problem may be present and you must visit the vet to get your cat checked out. This is also recommended for owners who suffer feline aggression and can't find the reasons behind it, or have an aggressive cat with other behavioural or physical symptoms.

Territorial Aggression

As you probably already know, cats are territorial creatures by nature. Though this type of aggression is more commonly seen happening between cats, it is known to happen from cat to human. Cats can also be selective about who they show territorial aggression to, so you may find some people in your household will be affected and some won't. New visitors will most likely be targets as they are the unknown and have unrecognised scents. Being calm and not confronting the cat will help. Allowing them to rub themselves against you will allow them to mark their scent and familiarise with you.

Aggression from Petting

Lots of cats love being stroked and handled. This cannot be said for all cats, however. Cats enjoy different things according to their preference and their mood. Some cats may become irritated by being handled and show aggression as a result. This is most common is repetitive petting and can be alleviated by keeping petting in moderation and giving your cat space, particularly those who generally take a disliking to being handled. If he wants affection he will come to you. Once you see a difference in posture, pupils, ears, ear position and tail, you might want to stop, in fact, it is highly recommended that you stop...

Maternal Aggression

A protective mother instinct is not exclusive towards other cats. Maternal aggression can also occur towards humans. The mother wants to keep any danger away from her kittens. People love kittens and just can't resist going near them to touch them or handle them. If they do this to kittens who are new-born they may face the wrath of the queen. Respect this natural instinct and try not to handle the kittens until the mother is more relaxed about you being near them.

Idiopathic Aggression

If every possible cause is ruled out and even examined by a professional, your cat may have idiopathic aggression. This can be quite disconcerting as the cat can be extremely aggressive and cause harm to you and others over and over again. The level of aggression is considered dangerous and you must discuss the problem with your vet. They will rule out all possible causes and perhaps look at other options such as behaviour training with a professional. You must be conscious of not only your safety but the cat's own health and happiness.

Behaviour of Stray and Feral Cats

Taking in a stray cat is different to attempting to take in a feral one. Stray cats have come from homes and would have gained the knowledge and socialisation required to behave appropriately and harmoniously in a home and around people. This is something they learn from a young age. For feral cats, however, it is quite different. Feral cats are more likely to have been born in the wild, which means it has not received the human handling required when it was a kitten – this handling is needed at around 7 to 8 weeks of age. A feral cat hasn't had this and will therefore not be too familiar or comfortable interacting with humans. If they cannot do this, it's wildly unrealistic to expect them to treat your house as their new home. Most cat experts and vets therefore advise against people attempting to 'domesticate' a feral cat. You may have better luck with a feral kitten, as long as they are younger than 8 weeks of age. Introducing gradual handling and socialisation may work with plenty of patience, but there is still a chance of hostile, fearful or aggressive behaviour – remember this is more and more likely to be the case the older the kitten is, so try your best to identify the age. Over 8 weeks and you may be causing more problems for the cat than solutions.

Adult feral cats may be seen by a vet and neutered to prevent future complications, but after this many vets advise the cat be returned to the wild. Though many other veterinary professionals feel this is abandoning them, others argue feral cats are still watched over by people who feed them and any attempts to keep them in homes as domesticated felines will almost always fail and affect their physical and mental welfare.

Cats Who Dislike Being Groomed

Another behavioural difficulty many cat owners face is a feline who highly dislikes being brushed, cleaned or claw-clipped. Cats that have been groomed since they were kittens will be far more adapted to the grooming process, so it is always recommended to introduce grooming during kittenhood and keep it a regular occurrence throughout the cat's life.

Cats are more likely to hate being groomed because they were never groomed from a young age and the experience feels unpleasant, giving them an uncomfortable feeling of being encroached upon. The feeling of grooming could be pleasurable for cats used to the experience, but for the unaccustomed it might have the opposite effect.

Long haired cats might be a little harder to groom than short haired ones. The process takes longer and the cat has to tolerate and feel it for longer. You need to reverse these feelings of dislike by introducing a highly enjoyable element to each and every grooming session – the obvious choice is food. Find a food your cat adores and only use it at grooming time. Give a small amount to your cat at the same time as grooming so they are fixed on the joys of the treat. Once it's gone, give them a tiny bit more and groom again. It's a bit by bit process.

Remember you must make it a positive experience, so pulling at mats and tangles with the brush will only cause discomfort and pain. Always stop if the cat shows signs of displeasure. Your cat may adjust better to a softer brush to begin with. If they get used to this, you can introduce other grooming tools later on.

A cat who behaves in the opposite fashion – a feline who grooms themselves excessively – may be showing signs of stress. Excessive licking can result in hair loss and skin problems. If you witness this you are better off speaking to your vet to find the possible cause behind it.

Compulsive Behaviour

Compulsive behaviour in cats involves repetitive habits that go beyond the normal healthy level of the activity towards an excessive level that interferes with everyday life and health.

Common signs of compulsive behaviour in felines include excessive eating, excessive grooming, repetitive movement such as pacing up and down, pica (eating inedible objects such as fabrics), constant licking, chewing fur and pulling at fur. Complications can occur from these habits, such as sore or wounded skin, hair loss, weight gain and internal obstructions from pica habits.

Some of the problems compulsive behaviour can cause affect the cat's health dramatically and this is not just physical health. Though we cannot know 100% what is going on in a cat's mind, we can look at what a compulsive disorder does to a human and note that a cat's mental health is affected in similar ways. Nobody wants their cat's quality of life to diminish because of a decline in both physical and mental health.

So, why does a cat suffer from a compulsive behaviour? It can start off when a cat is distressed or agitated, for example a frustrated cat who yearns to do something but cannot do it. If he can't do this thing he so sorely wants to do, he opts for another activity to take its place. This is called displacement behaviour.

It slowly becomes compulsive when a cat is repeatedly put in the situation where they can't do something and their frustration leads them to do something else instead, e.g. lick their fur or pace up and down. It starts off only happening in times of stress, but ends up happening even when there is no stress.

There are some factors that may contribute to the likelihood of a cat developing a compulsive behaviour: Indoor cats with less stimulation who are enclosed in places where stress can occur, female cats are sometimes more known to chew and bite at fur compulsively, specific breeds may have a slightly higher risk such as Siamese cats, younger cats and kittens are also more likely to develop compulsive habits, and cats who have experienced disruption and stress from being rehomed, moving home or having new members to the household.

Other factors could play a part, too. Every neighbourhood has cats wandering around. Cats outside the property near doors and windows could cause the continuous stress and frustration. Any triggers that cause fear or stress in your cat can also lead to compulsion. Loud noises, presence of children or regular house guests are common examples.

Many cat owners report their cat doing repetitive behaviour simply because they are bored and demand attention from their owners. This is normally down to a lack of stimulation at home.

Separation anxiety is another prime reason behind compulsive behaviour. Cats left alone for long periods of time or cats suddenly alone after the leaving or loss of a fellow animal or human can become repetitive, or even compulsively destructive, due to the anxiety.

Let's look at how to tackle the common compulsive behaviours and causes:

If it's a specific object your cat likes to eat, try and keep it out of their reach. If it's a permanent material or piece of furniture you can cover it up or stop your cat from entering the specific room it is in. Some objects can be sprayed with deterrent products, but be sure to ask your vet for safe recommendations. Cats may lose interest in chewing, sucking or eating fabrics in particular if you give them toys that match the same texture and material.

A cat being compulsive from stress brought on by a phobia or fear will ease away when the fear is addressed. Earlier in this book there is mention of fear in cats and what you can do to stop it – in particular, take note of the de-sensitisation and counterconditioning methods for decreasing fear and anxiety in your cat.

Cats stressed out by other cats within the household will benefit from being separated temporarily and reintroduced on a gradual basis later on. Reintroductions must be done calmly giving both cats freedom to enter and explore each other – also try and make this meeting enjoyable for both parties. Halt the proceedings if you see any signs of distress and continue with the separation for a little longer.

Cats stressed by cats outside should not be given full access to windows, patio doors or windowed doors looking out to the garden. If possible, cover them up and relocate any perching areas your cat has near windows and doors to somewhere where this view is not possible. Make these areas more enticing by adding blankets, toys and comforting surfaces. Being able to see other cats may frustrate an indoor cat and thus cause displacement behaviour that leads onto compulsion.

A permanently indoor cat requires plenty of exercise and stimulation. This may mean extra time playing with you and other people, as well as plenty of variety in the toys they have. Cats like to climb, so think about investing in a 'cat tree' where he can observe from a height and chill out. There are various interactive toys on the market designed for both lone play and play with the owner. Scratching structure and toys designed for stimulation of sight, sound, touch and smell are also advised.

Cats being compulsive with separation anxiety may also benefit from desensitisation and counterconditioning to prevent the anxiety causing the compulsion. De-sensitising a cat with separation anxiety will involve leaving them alone for very short periods of time to help ease the cat into adapting to being alone. Counterconditioning will involve making home alone time more pleasant instead of stressful with puzzles, activities, interactive long-play toys and so on. Additionally, close off the areas where compulsion and destruction occurs and invest in objects to distract your cat. If all else fails, crate training may help resolve the problem.

Sometimes cats may do compulsive habits in order to gain attention from their owners. Unfortunately, most people give in and shower their cat with attention when they do something compulsive. Some people do it without even realising they are simply because the cat's compulsive behaviour is worrying, annoying or potentially dangerous to the cat's health. Giving them the attention is, in fact, like a reward. They soon learn that doing their compulsive activity got them the attention they wanted and this just encourages them to keep doing it. Avoid attention and, instead, simply interrupt their habit with a clap, a firm command or use something to make a noise. If the cat's habit is chew or eating related, get rid of the item they are transfixed with at that moment.

Many of the solutions to compulsion are addressed in the fear, stress and anxiety sections of this book, since compulsive behaviour is heavily linked with these three problems. Cat owners often don't find out why their cat has a compulsive disorder and the underlying cause may need to be investigated by keeping a close eye on the where the cat is, what they are doing and what they are experiencing when the compulsion arises. You should also consult your vet about the matter, particularly in cases where all attempts to remedy the issue have failed, as they may be able to investigate for you or prescribe behavioural and anxiety medication. Always act on compulsive behaviour – your cat's welfare depends on it.

CHAPTER FOURTEEN
BEHAVIOUR TRAINING TIPS

Cats are trainable, but it may require slightly different techniques compared to training a dog because they are different species with similar, yet different instincts.

Severe behavioural problems need to be addressed by a veterinary professional with a possible referral to a behaviourist. If it's something you could fix at home, then try these behaviour training tips:

Patience and Understanding
First thing's first: Training takes lots of patience along with a thorough understanding that animals are animals and they are naturally inclined not to be like humans. We therefore cannot expect them to behave exactly like us and see the world in the same way. They will sometimes do things we wouldn't want them to do and we must accept we both operate differently and never become aggressive or lose patience when teaching them behaviour. Remember they are learning and will not become top cat overnight.

Punishment
It's common for people to assume that rewards entice cats to behave the way they want and punishment deters the cat from behaving undesirably. To think punishment has the same effectiveness as a reward is actually wrong. Rewards can work, but using punishment because you feel it has the same positive effects on correcting and teaching behaviour will do more harm than good. Punishment doesn't work the way many people think it does. Infact, it makes what you're trying to achieve less likely.

Any act of punishment will simply confuse and often scare or stress a cat. The impact of the punishment will put your cat into a mood and cause behaviour that makes the problem you're trying to solve worse. Your cat will become fearful and stressed and may avoid you because she may think it could happen again. Your cat may become confused because she will not necessarily associate what she did wrong with how you are reacting. So, though you probably already knew this, avoid punishment at all costs.

Learning How Your Cat Ticks for Effective Training

Before you even begin training your cat to behave you will need to grasp what exactly motivates them to do things. Cats as hunters will always appreciate food and this is a common driving force for training cats, so invest in some treats you know will be special for your cat. You could also think of other things – new toys, for example. Also make sure these foods or objects are given sparingly and are only used during training as a reward. Your cat will soon learn these rare treats are given when a certain action is achieved and not something given away willy-nilly. Never give in to pressure and give the treats away just because your cat pesters or begs you for them.

After progress is made you may start reducing the level of treats being given, but only when you start to notice your cat's trained behaviour becoming automatic. Also, it's nice every now and then to still give them a little something.

You must also think of training as a gradual process that, for your cat, should be considered a game involving steps – you start with very simple and easy ones and work your way up. If your cat thinks of training as a game they will be more likely to give you their attention.
This 'game' should also be a game your cat cannot lose. If they get something wrong you simply start it over again. You never punish the cat, but instead you encourage and reward when things are done right. Usually when a mistake is made, the person conducting the training should be held accountable – it just means you are going too quickly and need to slow down to your cat's learning pace.

Start When They're Kittens

Kittens are going through a life of learning and adapting to new things, so introducing training from a young age will probably be more effective than training an adult cat. Get them used to being handled first, then play games and interact more and more. Later you can start a gentle grooming regime which will help them adapt to such activities without problems emerging later in their life.

Potty Training

Kittens will inevitably have accidents. They have yet to become accustomed to expectations such as where to eliminate and their bladder control, much like puppies, won't be as good until a little bit later. It's important, then, to adopt a subtle potty training regime that makes alterations that encourage the kitten's behaviour to change from house soiling to going in the litter tray.

Any signs of a kitten eliminating in the house should be responded to by helping them associate elimination with a litter tray - take the kitten immediately to the litter tray when you witness this. If these unwanted house eliminations happen while you're away from home, keep them in one large, non-carpeted room with a bed, food and water on one side and a clean litter tray on the other. Keep these two areas separate as cats do not like eliminating near where they sleep and eat. Also keep the litter tray as easy to access as possible.

A smelly, dirty litter tray will make your kitten zero percent interested in eliminating there. Keep it clean, but a little scent within the box is desirable in order to teach them by scent that this is the area to urinate. Having additional litter trays is advisable and a multi-storey home will benefit from having one on each level. Being such a small cat will limit their physical ability to move long distances to just one tray. If you notice your kitten using the litter tray you should consistently reward them. Be sure to take note of the common times they eliminate, such as after meals or nap times. Also keep the kitten near the litter tray after meals. Maybe try taking them to the tray after their nap or meal as this is a likely time they will want to go.

Getting Your Cat to Sit

Getting your cat to sit will help in situations where he is not doing what he is supposed to – it's a good distraction and is also a reminder of who is in charge.

Grab the special treats and hold them in front of your cat's nose while they are standing. Slowly move the treats over his head to prompt your cat to raise their nose upwards and settle his rear down to the ground – he is now sitting. At this point you say "sit" as soon as he does and then give them the treat. When they scoff or take the treat from your hand you can say an encouraging phrase such as "good boy/girl". Repeat this process a few times a day and hopefully you will begin to notice your cat sitting whenever your hand is near their head – even an empty hand. Keep using the treats until the automatic response is kicking in and then you can start using them less and less. Always use words of encouragement, however.

Getting Your Cat to Stop

Being able to stop your cat in their tracks when they are doing something they shouldn't is extremely useful. Cats may be prone to poking their noses in drinks or attacking your legs, so having a method to control this behaviour is highly desirable, as well as showing your cat their behaviour in that moment is unacceptable.

Never use your cat's name when you command them to stop doing something. He will associate his name with negativity, so only use it when you praise him. Instead use firm, short words used in an assertive, but not aggressive, tone – "No" is a common choice. Use this word as soon as you witness the bad deed happening. If ignored, repeat the word while clapping your hands a few times. Get his attention and remove him from the area if further commands are ineffective. If he does stop when you say "no", be sure to reward him with encouraging words, affection, some play time or a treat. Whatever he likes the most! Be persistent with this as it may take some time to set in. This could become repetitive and somewhat irritating, but keep patient and never stop or have a break in your commands or you'll be back to square one.

A Cat That Needs to Get Down

Cats love exploring and climbing as this is a natural habit they enjoy. We, however, certainly do not appreciate it when they jump up on clean kitchen counters where food is prepared, get on coffee or dinner tables, climb up televisions or walk across shelves or surfaces where things are easily damaged or pushed off and broken. These are no-go kitty zones and rightly so. Start by realising why your cat does it in the first place. If she wants to climb and jump, give her enough opportunities to do so by getting climbing trees and perches – anything she knows is an acceptable thing to engage these activities with.

As you would when dealing with a cat doing something they shouldn't, use firm and assertive words to express to her she is wrong to jump up on this surface. The best one is "down!" or "off!" Use this every time you notice it happening immediately and repeat the phrase while clapping your hands loudly if she doesn't get the hint. Also change your body language. Never become aggressive or scary, but be assertive and use gestures such as pointing to the floor. Avoid using treats as a way of bribing the cat down to the floor as they will simply jump up on the surface more often in order to get treats.

Other ways to avoid this behaviour are indirect, such as storing any tempting foods or drinks away and not leaving any unattended. You can also make the surfaces unappealing to the cat by using citrus cleaners or leaving lemon or orange peel as a natural deterrent.

Teaching Your Cat to Stop Aggressive Responses

If you notice aggression, you should read the section on aggression in the problem behaviour chapter of this book first. It's important to find the reason behind such behaviour before finding out what can be done about it.

Playing with your cat is fun and adorable, but not so fun if your cat takes a swipe or bite at you. Cats may mock this behaviour any way, as play time naturally involves acting out their natural instincts. Cats will love attention and having the opportunity to engage in exciting play with you, so of course it will be not so fun for them if they sink their teeth or claws into your hands or feet and you stop the games. Stopping as soon as you are hurt is the best response, however. It gives a message plain and simple to your cat:

"When you do that, this happens" – "When you bite me, play time ends." It's not to punish the cat, but to help them associate those unwanted actions end a fun activity and exciting feeling and your cat doesn't want that.

For gentle play you need to praise your cat when he is being gentle and not using his claws or teeth, but just his paws. Use praising words such as "good boy" or "good girl". Test him by increasing the excitement of the game you are playing. If he starts showing signs of aggression by showing his teeth or claws or becoming overexcited, immediately stop the game or calm it down. If he calms down, you can continue playing with him. Any biting or scratching must be responded to just as another cat would – be vocal and yell something such as "Oww!" or "Ouch!", stop the game and leave the room while completely ignoring your cat. This is to be repeated until signs of improvement occur. Provide plenty of scratching posts or structures, various pouncing and chasing games and plenty of toys for chewing, biting, clawing and so on. This much-needed stimulation can help ease any aggression towards you during play.

Training Your Cat to Come When Called

It's always handy to teach your cat to come to you, whether it's for dinner time or to get them out of an area you don't want them in. Firstly, ensure you are a few metres away from your cat and call them by their name. She should turn around and look at you. Hold some treats in your hand and hold it out towards her, then bring it towards you and say the word "come" as soon as you notice your cat coming to you. Once she arrives, give the treats to her and tell her "good girl". Now move away slightly and hold a few more treats in your hand.

Call her name again and say "come" when your cat starts walking or running to you. This process should be repeated on a regular basis, but increase the distance between yourself and your cat more and more each time. When you progress, try the process with the cat looking away from you occupied with something. Always stop before your cat becomes bored and always use plenty of praise, particularly when you start to phase out the treats. Cats always need to be reassured they have

have done the right thing or the lesson could be unlearned.

Clicker Training

Otherwise known as operant conditioning, clicker training is a method that involves a cat's natural inclination to repeat something that they know has an enjoyable result.

A clicker is used to mark a wanted behaviour that will be rewarded. It is a device that makes a clicking noise unlike any other noise a cat would hear in their day to day life – it is distinct and clear. Eventually the cat will associate the clicking noise with the behaviour you want him to carry out, of which he will be particularly keen to repeat because of the positive outcome – the treats given after the click.

Start by getting the cat familiar with the clicking sound. Click to gain his attention and follow the click with a small treat. Don't use large quantities of a treat and use something he adores to eat as this will make him long for more. This may take some time depending on the cat, but once he properly connects the click with getting a treat you are ready to start using commands with the clicker.

Use commands such as "come" to begin with and notice he should come to you to be given the treat, but this can be used with other commands, too, and when done with patience and longevity it can progress to working on a number of different behaviours. Just be sure to start with little steps and easy accomplishments.

At advanced stages, you may even be able to gradually phase out the clicker and replace the clicking sound with a word or gesture. Phasing out treats can also occur later on as long as you always praise your cat every time he does what you asked.

CHAPTER FIFTEEN
THE MYTHS OF CAT BEHAVIOUR

Lots of behaviours we often associate with a meaning that, in the real world, is simply not true. Dispelling these tales brings you another step forward to understanding why cats do what they do.

Myth #1

Your Cat Will Definitely Hate Your Baby

That's a myth. It's not 100% guaranteed that your cat will take a liking to a new baby or not. Your cat is likely to treat a new-born baby with caution. Cats love the familiar and bringing a brand new, tiny human being back all of a sudden will be confusing for them. After a while they will learn to get used to them, but rarely do we hear of cats being aggressive towards babies. The fact is, your cat is probably more scared of the baby than you think.

Cats may even learn to welcome a young child into the home as part of their perceived "clowder" and it's often seen that cats are calmer and less vicious around babies and toddlers. Older children who haven't be taught how to behave around a cat are more at risk, especially if they pester the cat or wave their hands or feet in the cat's face to point where the cat is tempted to take a swipe.

To help the process, you can introduce your baby to the cat in small, monitoring meetings. Allow the cat to freely approach the baby, then sniff around and become acquainted. Keep the experience calm and pleasant for both parties and be sure to include some rewards for good behaviour.

Of course, it is entirely up to you whether you allow your cat to enter the baby's nursery or not.

Myth #2

Cats Prefer to Keep Themselves to Themselves

That's a myth. Yes, they like alone time and yes, they can keep themselves entertained, but they certainly require lots of interaction, attention and lots of play with their owners in order to be fully content and stimulated.

Lonely cats will be unhappy and depressed. A cat left alone too much risks getting separation anxiety, so always make time for your cat and keep plenty of toys at home. Make some activities for them to do while you're away and never assume they always want peace and quiet. Though cats are different socially to dogs, they still need to be social with you. Doing so with your cat will decrease chances of naughty, attention-grabbing behaviour.

Myth #3

Cats Possess Evil and Selfish Behaviour Compared to Dogs

Any cat owner will know this is a myth. Though dogs are known as man's best friend, cats are too often perceived as being manipulative, evil and less caring of their human owners than dogs and it's simply not correct. A healthy, well-looked after cat will thrive from human attention and adore affection. They will be affectionate in return. All cats are different, granted, but they collectively have different ways of showing their affection compared to dogs. You simply cannot compare the two.

Myth #4

Dogs Can Be Trained But Cats Can't

Myth – their behaviour can be trained to improve. Though it's not re alistic to train your cat to bring your slippers to you every morning, you can train them the house rules of what is acceptable and what is unacceptable. Obedience training is perfectly possible, with the use of certain words and tones associated with specific actions. You can also show your cat what happens when they misbehave – an innocent game could go wrong when your cat goes too far and nips your hand. They can learn to stop doing this when you withdraw all the attention they have been enjoying up to that point. They will then associate taking a nip with play time being over.

Myth #5

Cats Possess Evil and Selfish Behaviour Compared to Dogs

Any cat owner will know this is a myth. Though dogs are known as man's best friend, cats are too often perceived as being manipulative, evil and less caring of their human owners than dogs and it's simply not correct.

A healthy, well-looked after cat will thrive from human attention and adore affection. They will be affectionate in return. All cats are different, granted, but they collectively have different ways of showing their affection compared to dogs. You simply cannot compare the two.

Myth #6

All Cats Have Nine Lives

Myth – although you probably already knew that. This myth has likely originated from a very ancient tale and has no truth to it whatsoever. A cat can come across as rather invincible sometimes, particularly as they get involved in fights, jump long distances and often walk away unscathed after they fall off something. It's silly to assume they are indestructible, however, as cats get involved in fatal accidents all the time. Always treat your cat as a one-life animal, because they are.

Myth #7

All Cats Are Scared of Water

Myth. Some cats can't stand being forcefully emerged in water and you can't blame them. Many cats would otherwise be naturally seeking sources of fresh water from streams or rivers in the wild, so it's a little absurd to think they dislike the water.

In fact, certain breeds of cat are mesmerised by water and are often seen licking at taps and trying their hardest to get some droplets from bathtubs or sinks. Some cats also like to go fishing for their next meal and can also enjoy swimming - the Turkish Van breed for example.

Myth #8

Cats Scratch Because They Are Aggressive

Myth. Some cats with aggressive behavioural problems may scratch, but then cats can scratch for various reasons. A cat who hasn't been trained or taught right from wrong may be more inclined to scratch, but often scratching can be associated with natural behaviour. Cats scratch furniture, carpets or materials because they need to sharpen their claws and remove old husks.

They also do it as a form of exercise to tone their muscles in order to move and hunt effectively. Or they could be trying to tell you something such as "pay attention to me" or "that's frustrating, leave me alone". Sometimes a cat will scratch because they have an underlying medical condition and feel agitated by it. Invest in scratching posts, cover furniture, use obedience commands and redirect your cat to toys if scratching occurs. Indoor cats may need their claws clipped carefully with a special claw clipper, but the option of declawing is cruel and not legal in the UK.

Myth #9

If a Cat is Purring it Definitely Means it's Happy

It's a myth to assume this. It's likely a cat will purr if you're stroking him and giving him attention and yes, that does mean he is content and enjoying the experience. He could also be communicating to you in this way. However, you cannot assume a cat purr is always a sign of happiness. Many cats purr when they are in poor health and when they are stressed. This could be to warn others to keep away and leave them be, or could be used as a method to comfort themselves when feeling ill or in pain. Similarly, mothers purr to their kittens to comfort them and communicate to them during a time where they are vulnerable and haven't fully developed their senses.

Myth #10

Cats All Behave The Same

Myth. That's like saying all humans behave the same, and everyone knows that is not true.

Cats, like people, have individual personalities. Those owning more than one cat will be able to notice quite clearly how differently cats behave. Some are shy, some are assertive, some are daredevils, some are chilled out, some adore people and children, some love sitting on laps, some love sitting beside you, some don't … the list could go on forever.

This is also one of many reasons why people are advised to check out a litter before choosing a kitten. Apart from observing how the litter interact with their mother and how healthy they are, you can also get a glimpse of all the personalities and which ones you click with. It's often said cats are like furry humans! Their traits are versatile and extremely enjoyable and lovable.

CHAPTER SIXTEEN
FREQUENTLY ASKED QUESTIONS

So many questions pop up in veterinary clinics and hospitals regarding cat behaviour. It's always less confusing for cat owners to know what and why something is happening when it happens. This chapter will highlight some of the most asked questions to help you find the reasons behind cat behaviour.

Why does my cat attack and bite me?

Trust can diminish when you're doing something enjoyable with your pet cat and they suddenly lash out by attacking and biting at you or others. However, it's important to remember cats are naturally and instinctively wired to be playful, to be predators and to be social. Things become a real problem when this aggression leads to unnecessary attacks on people.

If your cat attacks you when you're stroking and comforting them it can be confusing. The cat is likely to be conflicted with the feelings of: 1) Feeling relaxed and satisfied by the petting, and 2) Realising that being too relaxed makes them vulnerable – a survival instinct kicking in. This could explain why they suddenly show aggression during a calm and enjoyable activity. Any signs of aggression mentioned earlier in this book will be present before the aggression materialises, so watch out for them to avoid an unpleasant experience!

Cats are often known to attack their owners during play time, too – another situation where you would think they are in good spirits. Kittens often learn when they become a little too aggressive during play through reactions from other cats. Cats may become too excited during play and the constant movement of close hands and feet of humans become a tempting target for rough play. Withdrawal of your hands and feet is encouraged, with the use of toys instead to teach the cat which things are okay to tackle with.

It's all about showing them what is acceptable to play with and what isn't, whether it's through toys or with some behavioural training involving firm commands and withdrawal of play time when things get too much. Obviously punishment simply causes the behaviour to worsen and confuses the cat, so always remember it's a patient learning process.

It's not always immediately clear why a cat attacks. There are various reasons behind this behaviour, such as frustration due to lack of stimulation and attention, aggression out of fear or anxiety, or even a sign your cat is ill and doesn't want to be bothered. If the behaviour persists you are best to visit your vet who will investigate the exact problem.

Why does my cat meow or vocalise excessively?

The opening chapters of this book explain the various vocalisations cats engage in and what they mean. Often, though, these vocalisations can be excessive and owners are baffled as to why. It could be for a perfectly natural and normal reason, but sometimes it's not.

Cats can vocalise a lot when they are hungry. Every cat owner knows how cats adore meal times and they will communicate and encourage their owners to fill their food bowl. A cat that vocalises and grabs for your attention in this way after meal times may need to be seen by a vet, as they should calm down after a feed.

A female cat that hasn't been spayed will be extremely vocal when "on heat". This is because she is calling and there's little you can do to stop it apart from calming her down by keeping her to a fixed part of the home or, if you don't want a litter from her, a simple solution is getting her spayed.

Cats or kittens can be more vocal than usual if their environment or routine has changed recently. This could be anything from being re-homed, having members of their cat family taken away, moving house, new pets being added to the household or the loss or arrival of new people to the household. It should ease off as soon as your cat adapts to the changes. Taking steps to make them comfortable and surrounding them with familiar objects will help.

Being so territorial, a cat could vocalise a lot because of 'outside' cats entering what they perceive to be their territory. Think about where your cat vocalises – by a door or window where they can look outside? Outside in the garden or neighbourhood? Are there other cats around? Keep them apart and block any view your cat may have of outside creatures.

Cats, particularly certain breeds, thrive from regular company from their humans. A clingy cat will vocalise and meow a lot more when he's not getting the attention he needs. If your cat is left alone in part of the house he can get lonely. If he can't find you or you're shut off from him he is more likely to vocalise for attention. More attention, play time and affection is required more regularly.

Excessive vocalisation isn't always connected with healthy and normal behaviour. Cats can become vocal when they experience ongoing pain or aren't very well for whatever reason. If your cat's vocalisations are accompanied with lethargy, vomiting, diarrhoea, problems with mobility or any other signs of illness or unusual behaviour, take them to your vet as soon as you can.

Why does my cat eat grass?

A cat that is fed a balanced diet leaves their owner puzzled when caught eating grass or plants. The truth is there is no certain reason why cats can be drawn to consuming grass, but it's actually considered quite normal for cats to occasionally eat small amounts of greenery. Many theories suggest cats eat grass and plants purely for fun or stimulation. The outside world can be exciting for a cat and chewing at some leaves can become a hobby of sorts. This is particularly the case for cats who feel the need to chew on a regular basis. The texture of plants could satisfy their chewing needs. Maybe some more textural chew toys are in order.

Another theory suggests cats eat plants and grass in order to be sick, which would then ease any gastrointestinal problems they are suffering from. The same technique may also work for cats wishing to be sick to clear any hairballs making them uncomfortable.

Some cats suffer from "pica". Mentioned earlier in this book, pica is when a cat develops an unusual habit of licking, chewing, biting or eating inedible objects. The cause is often unknown, but could be down to poor diet, stress, a compulsive disorder, lack of stimulation or simply because it generates a pleasing feeling. Keep an eye out for the risk of poisoning, sickness, choking or internal obstructions from pica habits. It's best to keep the favourite item away from the cat and improve their diet and overall lifestyle.

Keep an eye out for your cat showing interest in plants known to be poisonous to cats, as well as plants sprayed with chemicals. Signs of illness should be reported to a vet.

Why does my cat bring home dead animals?

It is understandably unpleasant to be greeted by your cat and realise they have come back with a dead bird or rodent in their mouth or placed in their bowl. The thing we often forget, though, is that cats are natural predators who are wired to hunt for survival. This is therefore a perfectly natural instinct for a cat regardless of how much home life he has. People assume feeding their cat more food will stop the behaviour. This is unlikely to ease their natural hunting desire.

It's suggested that cats can bring home dead prey because they have an instinct to show their hunting capabilities and feed their "clowder". Another reason could be they simply bring home their catch because it's a safe place to leave it to eat later without other cats taking possession. It could even be said our cats are showing us how to hunt effectively, harking back to the "clowder" behaviours where our cat thinks we have hunting instincts just like he does.

Bringing back dead or alive prey may stem from when the cat was a kitten and his mother showed him how to hunt and what to do with prey. Many behaviourists suggest this taught habit along with a natural instinct is more likely to be the reason behind bringing home dead animals as opposed to the "gift" theory – a theory that claims cats bring home animals as a token for their owners.

Regardless of the reason, it's very difficult to stop such a natural behaviour. Try not to punish your cat or show anger over their little outing souvenir. Offering him some puzzle toys or wearing a collar with a bell attached may help to some extent. Accepting his dead offering and disposing of it discreetly is the best response.

Why does my cat drink from taps?

It can get tedious when your cat jumps up on kitchen counters or climbs up bathroom sinks or bathtubs to drink from taps. Even when they are not dripping a cat can lick away in hope of catching a few droplets to drink. The obvious reason would be because they are dehydrated and are simply not getting enough fresh water – water that is changed at least twice a day. However, most cat owners give their cat all the water they could need and still have a cat who is a tap enthusiast.

It could just be your cat isn't happy with drinking water from a bowl. Certain breeds in particular, for example Bengals, adore fresh running water which they would have naturally obtained in the wild before being domesticated. Taps can provide this – a bowl of old water can't. Cats have been known not to naturally understand why food bowls and water bowls are put together because they deem these two activities as being separate. A way to change this would be to place fresh water somewhere away from the food area.

Though drinking from an old tap in an area where human food isn't prepared is fine to allow, most cats also go for kitchen or bathroom taps – places and surfaces they will turn into unhygienic environments by licking, sitting and walking on. This needs to be discouraged. Though stopping a cat drinking from taps completely is tricky, you could provide the same fresh running water a cat is attracted to with cat fountains. Have a little research and, if you can afford it, invest in a cat drinking fountain.

Why does my cat hate going to the vets?

Being put into a pet container, being in a loud and moving car or being walked along a loud street to the veterinary clinic can be daunting for a cat. Even more so when they have to sit in the waiting room with various other animals, some of which are vocal and five times bigger, and various smells and movement sensations are experienced. It's pretty easy for your cat to be alarmed, fearful and scared of noises, other animals and the vet themselves. And, of course, there's having to be handled and having various procedures or examinations such as booster vaccinations, getting their temperature taken and so on.

Cats get edgy and frightened when they are taken out of a familiar and comforting environment and are put straight into an unknown one. Their natural instinct may kick in and cause them to become defensive and alert. They are also anxious because they can no longer predict what will happen as their usual environment disappears along with their usual routine.

Some cats can get used to being taken away from home for whatever reason, especially if it's a regular occurrence and has been happening since they were a kitten. Vet appointments, however, are normally only once a year for healthy cats just for check-ups and booster jabs, so it's hard for them to know what's going on each time.

Leave your cat to freely become acquainted with the pet carrier way before she is due to leave for the vets. Often such an inquisitive creature will love to explore and hang out in boxes like this. Maybe even try adding a few treats, a blanket and some toys to the box, particularly for the vet visit. Anything that will comfort them and remind them of the familiar. A noisy, busy vet waiting room full of big and unknown animals and people could frighten your cat, so if it's at all possible, ask reception when you book your appointment if they can slot you in at a quieter and less busy time of day. If a busy waiting room is avoidable, try not to get your cat out of their carrier while waiting.

If you have to drive to the vet you may notice your cat will also dislike the car journey. It will help if your cat is already familiar with the carrier first and, again, has familiar objects to occupy and comfort themselves with. Try starting out by taking your cat on short drives and seeing how they cope. Kittens will often learn to tolerate the movements and unknown atmosphere of a car much better.

Why does my cat beg for food?

It's confusing why a cat would beg for food, whether human food or cat food, despite the fact we feed them regularly. Cats have that instinct within them to survive, so it's natural for them as "hunters" to be fixated on when and where their next meal will come from.

Firstly, we have to figure out whether they are genuinely begging to be fed or whether we're mistaking their behaviour for something else. Cats can act in similar ways when they are feeling playful and want attention from you. See if they react to toys or playful behaviour from you and see where their focus is. If they rush to their bowl every time you walk by or try to break into food containers then you're right to assume it's food begging, particularly when they get under your feet, rub against you or vocalise.

Think about how you feed your cat. Is there diet high quality and balanced? Does it contain all the nutrients a cat needs to be healthy? If you're really not sure, ask your vet and they may be able to recommend some diet improvements or food recommendations.

How often do you feed your cat? And at what point in the day? Is it evenly spaced or does your cat have to endure a longer gap before being fed again? Often people will sit down for dinner before their cat has been fed for the evening – the smells and temptation of human food will prompt your cat to beg for scraps. A simple fix would be to feed your cat before you commence with your own breakfast or dinner. Also avoid giving them scraps from the table as this will encourage them to beg every time.

If it's still a problem during your meals, try taking your cat to a quieter part of the house and let them back out again once meals are finished and cleared away. Any food left out will become a temptation.
Two, evenly spaced meals a day should be adequate, but cats will appreciate a fresh bowl of water at all times and a bowl of biscuits so they can ease any mild hunger they feel during the day or through the night.

Cats seem to be very talented at convincing us to feed them. Many cat owners experience their cat begging in a way where they think twice about whether they actually fed them or not. Many cats like to act as if they haven't been fed… when they have! The intelligence of a cat can be so much so that they learn how you react to their behaviour. If you always give in, your cat will always beg, even when they are being fed properly and don't need more food.

In some cases, cats will beg for food because their appetites have intensified. Medical conditions can cause increased appetites, such as hyperthyroidism or diabetes, so be sure to check for any other unusual symptoms or behaviours and get them checked by your vet to rule any health problems out. Your vet will also need to see your cat if they are over or underweight.

Does my cat's behaviour change when she is sick?

Though cats can be notoriously good at masking their problems, any kind of ill health could be present in how she behaves. Symptoms are obvious signs of ill health: vomiting, lethargy, diarrhoea or constipation, swelling, limping, discharge from anywhere on the body, poor mobility, tarry stools, excessive scratching, excessive vocalisation, loss of appetite, increased or decreased urination and thirst, elimination out of the litter tray, anxiety, reluctance to communicate, weight loss or gain, bloody urine, difficulty breathing, and various other abnormal symptoms are indicators your cat is sick and needs medical attention.

Cats behaving differently to what you know is normal is a good indicator they are ill. You should know your cat better than anyone else, so it should be easy to spot.

Physical appearance can change when a cat is unwell – the coat may change if your cat is infested with parasites, is stressed and chews clumps of fur, is suffering from poor nutrition or has a poor health that hinders them from wanting to groom themselves.

A cat may have a different gait – unsteady, wobbly, limping, slow or stiff. All indicators of injury or trauma, or a medical condition such as osteoarthritis.

Plenty of cat owners notice their feline is unwell because they can see their "third eyelid" – A pink layer around the eye that isn't normally visible unless a cat isn't feeling well.

Habits can change. A cat who knows to urinate in their litter tray may suddenly start urinating where it shouldn't. Any learned activities such as this suddenly stopping is an indicator something could be wrong. Your cat's mood may become noticeably different. A happy and playful cat may become sluggish and not interested in physical attention. They may even reject any kind of attention from you and want to be left alone. Some cats show an out-of-character aggressiveness because they are ill and want to be left by themselves. Their mood might become a little strange or "crazy", with compulsive habits developing. Anything like this needs to be evaluated by a vet.

Why do cats' behaviour change with catnip?

We've all seen the effects of catnip. Cats seem to go crazy for it and behave hyperactive and excited. But what is it and how does it make our cats go mad for it?

Catnip is actually part of the mint family. An essential oil in catnip causes cats to react the way they do when they experience it. It's called nepetalactone. Your cat takes in the catnip scent and this is when the effect begins. Unfortunately, there is not enough research to be 100% certain on why it impacts a cat's mood. Some say the herb simply impersonates a happy pheromone that makes the cat's brain respond in such a way. Some cats are particularly sensitive to catnip, while others don't respond to it at all. This sensitivity has been known to be inherited, too.

Why does my cat suddenly "freak out" for five minutes?

Cat owners often report that their cat's normal behaviour will suddenly change very quickly into a burst of physical energy and vocalisation. The cat will start pouncing around and speeding around the house in a fit of madness almost as if it's being possessed. After a few minutes they return to normal.

Domesticated cats are not normally faced with the everyday life of wild cats. Though their natural instinct is to hunt their prey, explore the wild, climb rocks, stalk animals and similar habits, they don't always get the opportunity to do this at home. All this energy is therefore not used up and your cat may want to let out any excess by playing around. There is no need to worry, but a bit of play time with some toys to pounce and chase could help keep their energy levels from getting too high.

Why is my cat suddenly not eating?

It's common for cats to be less interested in their food bowl every now and then. This could be something harmless, such as hot weather, poor cleanliness, or not being too keen on a new pet food you've purchased. It becomes a more serious matter, however, if it persists for several days. A cat not eating at all needs a swift visit to the vet before lack of food affects their health.

Loss of appetite is a common symptom for a variety of health problems, from dental disease, gastrointestinal problems, worms, kidney disease, anxiety, depression, cancer and a large number of other illnesses varying from mild issues to very serious ones.

Some cats lose their appetite if they have recently had a vaccination, have travelled in a car and are suffering from motion sickness or have had a change in their environment or routine. A diet change can trigger a lack of interest in food as cats are often rather fastidious.

Persistent poor appetite or poor appetite present with other symptoms has to be checked by your vet as soon as possible. Cats, obviously, need to eat regularly. They are more fragile than humans and the problem needs to be addressed quickly. The best cure is finding the underlying reason for your cat not eating and finding it swiftly.

CONCLUSION

~

Many aspects of feline behaviour are not fully understood by humans. We tend to judge the intelligence of any animal by comparing its responses to our own. This is not an accurate way to compare the innate intelligence of any breed of animal.

Cats have their own inborn instincts that are very much a part of their life. The feral cat may have to rely on her hunting instincts, but your domestic cat uses the same motions and movements when she plays with her toys.

Cats have always been somewhat mysterious to people, since they don't do things like dogs do. We understand dog behaviour more easily. Perhaps it is this mystique that leads us to adopt cats into our lives, to learn more about them. Dogs can learn tricks a lot more quickly than cats, but this is because dogs are pack animals and they want to please the pack leader. In domestic life, this leader is their master or owner.

Whether cats are indeed aloof, or simply acting on their base instincts, will probably always be a topic of discussion among cat people – and dog people. However, if you have welcomed a cat into your heart, you know that she cares for you in her own way.

RESOURCES

- http://www.mnn.com/family/pets/stories/cat-sounds-and-what-they-mean
- http://www.a-house-full-of-cats.com/catsounds.html
- http://www.bandofcats.com/21-cat-behaviours-32-cat-sounds-and-their-secret-meaning/
- http://pets.webmd.com/cats/features/cat-body-language
- http://www.catster.com/cat-behaviour/cat-body-language
- http://www.humanesociety.org/animals/cats/tips/cat_communication.html
- http://www.aspca.org/pet-care/virtual-pet-behaviourist/cat-behaviour/socializing-your-kitten
- http://www.petparents.com/show.aspx/cats/cat-behaviour/socializing-cats
- http://www.tenthlifecats.org/all-about-cats/cat-behaviour/shy-cat-socialisation
- http://www.straightdope.com/columns/read/1143/do-cats-always-land-unharmed-on-their-feet-no-matter-how-far-they-fall
- http://www.physlink.com/education/askexperts/ae411.cfm
- http://www.perfectpaws.com/help1.html
- http://www.a-house-full-of-cats.com/catscentcommunication.html
- http://www.petplace.com/cats/why-do-cats-rub-up-against-things/page1.aspx
- http://animalendocrine.blogspot.com/2011/10/daily-water-requirements-and-needs-for.html
- http://www.catinfo.org/
- http://www.petmd.com/cat/behaviour/evr_ct_why_do_cats_knead
- http://healthypets.mercola.com/sites/healthypets/archive/2012/05/02/cat-kneading-behaviour.aspx
- http://animal.discovery.com/pets/cat-intelligence.htm
- http://www.messybeast.com/intelligence.htm
- http://www.icatcare.org/advice/cat-behaviour
- https://www.aspca.org/pet-care/virtual-pet-behaviorist/cat-behavior